YARN*play*

YARN*play*

LISA *shobhana* MASON

NORTH LIGHT BOOKS
CINCINNATI, OHIO

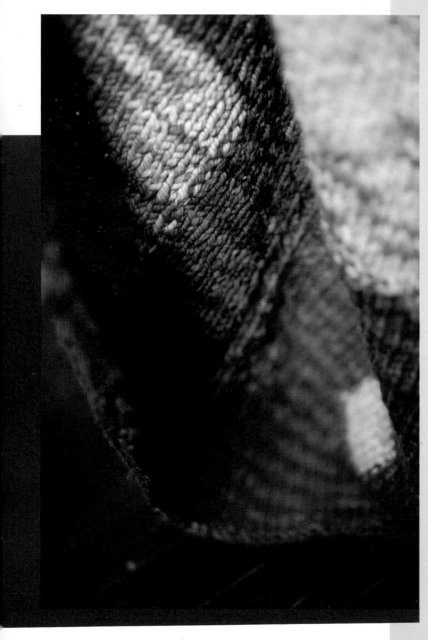

10 09 08 07 06   5 4 3 2 1

Distributed in Canada by Fraser Direct
100 Armstrong Avenue
Georgetown, ON, Canada L7G 5S4
Tel: (905) 877-4411

Distributed in the U.K. and Europe by David & Charles
Brunel House, Newton Abbot, Devon, TQ12 4PU, England
Tel: (+44) 1626 323200, Fax: (+44) 1626 323319
Email: postmaster@davidandcharles.co.uk

Distributed in Australia by Capricorn Link
P.O. Box 704, S. Windsor, NSW 2756 Australia
Tel: (02) 4577-3555

Library of Congress Cataloging-in-Publication Data

Mason, Lisa Shobhana.
  Yarnplay / Lisa Shobhana Mason. -- 1st ed.
    p. cm.
  Includes index.
  ISBN-13: 978-1-58180-841-4 (alk. paper)
  ISBN-10: 1-58180-841-0
  1. Knitting. 2. Knitting--Patterns. I. Title.
  TT820.M35 2006
  746.43'2043--dc22

                          2006015813

EDITOR: **JESSICA GORDON**
DESIGNER: **KARLA BAKER**
PHOTOGRAPHERS: **BRIAN STEEGE AND TIM GRONDIN**
ILLUSTRATIONS: **AMY TIPTON**
WARDROBE STYLIST: **MONICA SKRZELOWSKI**
SET STYLIST: **JAN NICKUM**
HAIR AND MAKEUP: **CASS SMITH**
PRODUCTION COORDINATOR: **GREG NOCK**

F+W PUBLICATIONS, INC.

This book is lovingly dedicated to the memory of my great-great aunt, Ruth Agnes Woods.

acknowledgments

Thanks to my one and only teacher, Lisa R. Myers, for never telling me that a project was too difficult to take on.

To Debbie Stoller, Vickie Howell and Tricia Waddell, thank you for believing in my vision and for giving me the opportunity to share my passion with knitters near and far. To Alexandra Virgiel and Jessica Gordon, your magic made it work!

Thanks to all of my fabulous knitblog friends for your encouragement, support and well-timed care packages of yarn, tea and chocolate!

To my students at Hill Country Weavers, thanks for showing up and giving me the opportunity to share my insane love for knitting with you!

Thanks to Artyarns, KFI, Lana Knits, Lion Brand, Lorna's Laces, Peace Fleece, South West Trading Company, Tahki Stacy Charles, and Westminster Fibers for your generous yarn support and willingness to accommodate last minute requests and changes.

Thanks to my mother Sharon Fields for always supporting me in all my endeavors.

To Gurumayi, thanks for lighting the path.

Thanks to David Bowie for making music to knit to, frog to and cast on to and knit to again! I think I know all the words to "Hunky Dory" and "Aladdin Sane" now...

Thanks to the everyday muses I pass on the street, women with a fearless sense of style who inspire me to push the envelope and to expand my ideas about what looks good.

And a very, very special thanks to Melissa Sternberg for not only knitting many of these projects, but for acting as a sounding board for my ideas and for continuing to listen when I had nothing to talk about beyond this book! Thanks for always being there and generously offering your support, your knowledge and your needles. I also want to thank the rest of the incredible women who knitted many of these projects and helped me to manifest my dream: Karli Capps, Valerie Lanford, Debra Marvin and Sara Wells.

contents

PLAYING
with $yarn$

Wearing, gifting and decorating with my handknits is my motivation for designing. I'm always excited to wear a sweater I've made or to put a handmade cushion on display in my living space. My work is highly personal. My knitted pieces reflect who I am and grow out of my inspirations, but they are also universal because they can be worn by both young and old, the fashion savvy and the more classic dressers.

My inspiration comes from many and varied sources—everything from outsider art to fashion icons and teenagers brings me a new and fresh idea.

I particularly take inspiration from the Gee's Bend quilters and outsider artists from the American South who create amazing art from whatever materials are at hand. Like their work, mine is intuitive. For me, knitting is a meditative practice during which I allow my spirit to guide me as I choose what color comes next or how to embellish a finished piece. I just let go and release my ideas of what I think the project should look like. You will be surprised at how much fun it can be to knit intuitively. Try letting your instincts guide you by working only with the skeins in your stash to make the Everything But the Kitchen Sink striped sweater on page 102. Or you can decide where and how often to place design elements in the Lorelei tank top (page 94) or the Poppy v-neck pullover (page 98).

I am also inspired by old school fashion designers like Vivienne Westwood, Yohji Yamamato, and Comme des Garcons, whose innovative use of fabric and shapes challenges and changes the very definition of fashion. Similarly, I like to turn things inside out, upside down, and on their sides to find a new way of doing things. I don't mind making mistakes because I know a mistake can be the beginning of a new design element.

I also draw inspiration from pop culture. I'm constantly exploring both new and old music, film and art, as well as the icons behind these creations. These influences saturate my consciousness and occasionally make their way into my designs (check out the asymmetrical Edie cardigan on page 86.)

Inspiration is never hard to find. When I am feeling creatively challenged I check out what my teenaged friends are wearing. They often have their finger on the pulse of what's hot on the streets. (The Austin Armwarmers, on page 52, are totally something my younger pals would wear!)

Of course, although creating knitted designs to fit your own personal inspirations is great, you can't put the cart before the horse. My philosophy is to first get a firm grasp on the basics of knitting. Understand that there is a "right way" and there are "other ways." Perfect the right way to do things to the best of your ability, and then loosen your hold and allow yourself to pursue "other ways." Now, by "other ways" I don't mean complex knitting acrobatics or trying to reinvent a simple stockinette. Rather, experiment with other ways of piecing together garments, where designs are placed, how a marriage of unexpected colors can create a vibrant new feeling, or how adding unexpected texture makes a design pop.

My style incorporates elements of couture and craft in a way that reflects my individuality, sense of humor, and need for comfort. I invite you to work loosely with these designs and color schemes, following your own inner wisdom to create a piece that is uniquely you!

EASY

INTERMEDIATE

ADVANCED

skill level
GUIDE

If you know the basics of knitting, you'll have no problem
following any of the patterns in this book. Some of the projects
are very, very simple, requiring just one stitch. Other projects
require a few different stitches and techniques. Each project
has an icon to let you know the required skill level.

1 STAR   All you need to know is knit and purl.

2 STARS   Up the ante a little: knitting and purling plus
               sewing seams together, doing a yarn over
               and/or working in the round. You'll also need
               to know techniques like simple crochet and
               picking up stitches.

3 STARS   Requires some fancy skills, like using a cable
               needle, following a chart or exercising your
               design skills.

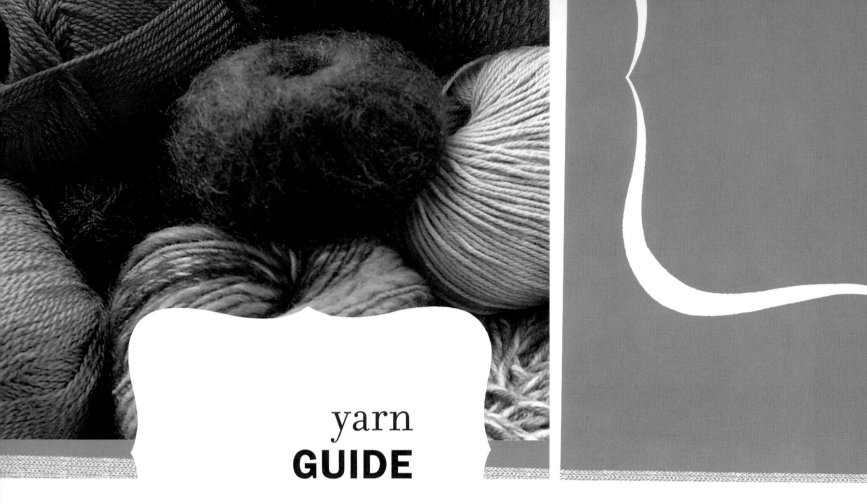

yarn
GUIDE

Ultimately, the quality of a garment is only as good as the yarn with which it's knit. I prefer to work with natural fibers because they look great, and feel good against your skin too. With the vast range of yarns available today, there is something to fit the taste, needs and budget of every knitter.

Before you venture into the wide world of yarn, there are just a few things you should know. It's very important to pick the fiber type, weight and texture that's right for the piece you're making.

A HANK, A SKEIN OR A BALL

Yarn can come in a loose hank, in a skein or in a ball.

A *hank* is yarn that's been loosely looped and then twisted and tied. It must be wound into a ball before you can knit with it. You can wind it by hand or with a swift and ball winder. Many yarn stores will wind a hank for you at no charge.

A *skein* of yarn is oblong in shape, and the free end is usually drawn from its center, which keeps the yarn from rolling around.

A *ball* of yarn is, well, a ball. It's round, and the free end is usually on the outside, which means it will do a fair bit of rolling.

ANIMAL, VEGETABLE OR SYNTHETIC

Fibers fall into three categories: animal, vegetable or synthetic.

Animal fibers include alpaca, angora, camel hair, cashmere, llama, mohair, silk and wool. These fibers come in all weights, colors and price ranges. Wool in particular is the staple of knitting fibers, and is often quite affordable. Sweaters, scarves and hats are good projects to make with wool.

Vegetable fibers include cotton, hemp and linen. These lighter-weight and breathable fibers are great for summer clothing.

Synthetics include acrylic, polyamide and polyester. These are generally the most affordable yarns. Acrylic yarn is great for baby projects because it can be machine washed and dried.

GENERAL GUIDELINES FOR YARN WEIGHTS

a **SUPER BULKY** up to 11 sts = 4" (10cm)

b **HEAVY WORSTED** 16 sts = 4" (10cm)

c **CHUNKY/BULKY** 12–15 sts = 4" (10cm)

d **FINGERING/SOCK WEIGHT** 28 sts = 4" (10cm)

e **ARAN/WORSTED WEIGHT** 18–20 sts = 4" (10cm)

f **SPORT WEIGHT** 24 sts = 4" (10cm)

g **DK WEIGHT** 21–22 sts = 4" (10cm)

h **LACE WEIGHT** 32+ sts = 4" (10cm)

WEIGHING THE OPTIONS
Yarn can be ultra-fine or super-thick. Or thick-and-thin. Make sure to pick a yarn that's the same weight as the yarn given for the pattern you're using. When it comes to yarn weight, the standards are not set in stone.

needle **GUIDE**

Before you cast on for any project, make sure you have the right
needles. Having the correct needle size for the yarn you're
working with is key to achieving the correct gauge. You may
choose needles made from any material you like. Here's a guide
to choosing the best needle for you.

SUGAR AND SPICE

Knitting needles come in such varied styles and colors, you could make a veritable bouquet with a colorful selection. Needles are made from all sorts of materials, inlcuding metal, plastic, casein, wood, bamboo and bone.

METAL NEEDLES are usually made from aluminum. They're super slippery, and the slickest variety can make your knitting quite speedy.

PLASTIC NEEDLES are often the most lightweight and economical choice. They're slightly more slippery than bamboo needles.

CASEIN NEEDLES are made from a milk protein. They're slightly flexible and are less slippery than metal needles.

BAMBOO OR WOOD NEEDLES "grab" the yarn, keeping stitches steady.

SHAPELY STICKS

Take your pick from tiny toothpick-sized needles to jumbo turkey-baster-sized needles. The weight of your yarn and the gauge of the project determine if you need a teensie-tiny size 000 or an enormous size 50 (or somewhere in between, more likely). There are straight needles, circular needles and double-pointed needles. Knitters often use more than one type of needle for one project, depending on the nature of the piece.

STRAIGHT NEEDLES are essentially long or short sticks with a knob or a flat circle at one end to keep the stitches from sliding off. They are used to knit flat pieces of fabric, and they work best for projects that are small to medium in size.

DOUBLE-POINTED NEEDLES (DPNS) have a point at each end, and they come in a set of four or five. They are used for knitting in the round. Stitches are distributed evenly over three or four of the needles, and the remaining needle is used to work the stitches. Double-pointed needles are especially handy for working small things in the round, like the tops of hats, or socks.

CIRCULAR NEEDLES are attached to each other with a flexible plastic cord. The connecting cord can be short or long. Use circular needles to knit in the round or to knit flat pieces. They are especially handy if you're knitting a large project, like an afghan, because they allow the weight of the knitted object to rest in your lap, versus being supported by your wrists and hands.

DOUBLE-POINTED NEEDLES
bamboo dpns and a fat crochet hook

CIRCULAR NEEDLES
plastic and bamboo circular needles

STITCH HOLDERS: Some are like safety pins without the sharp point. Others open on both ends for easy access. They come in all sizes and allow you to slide stitches off of your needles and keep them neatly in place.

TAPE MEASURE: A flexible cloth or plastic tape measure is invaluable to a knitter.

DARNING (YARN) NEEDLE: This is a blunt-tipped needle with a large eye to accommodate yarn. Use a darning needle to sew seams together.

RING MARKERS: These little circles of plastic slide onto your knitting to help you keep track of important spots in your knitting—like the beginning of a round.

RUSTPROOF LOLLIPOP OR T-PINS: These large straight pins are great for securing pieces for blocking.

CABLE NEEDLES: These small needles can be U-shaped or candy-cane-shaped. Choose a cable needle that is approximately the same size as the needles you're using for the main part of the project.

CROCHET HOOKS: Just like knitting needles, these hooks come in lots of different sizes. Buy a selection and use them to help you pick up dropped stitches and to make crochet borders.

tool
GUIDE

The proper array of tools is essential to fun and pain-free knitting. Here are some of the notions you will need.

STITCH GAUGE: This is a little square of plastic with ruled numbers on the sides and an L-shaped cutout along two ruled edges. You can lay the stitch gauge over your knitted swatch and count how many stitches and how many rows fit inside the cutout. Then divide the number of stitches by the number of inches (how

long and wide the cutout is) and you've calculated your gauge.

POINT PROTECTORS: These are little eraser-like plastic pieces that slide onto the pointed ends of needles to keep stitches from sliding off.

ROW COUNTER: This small plastic tube has rotating numbers (kind of like on a combination lock) that let you keep track of your rows.

SCISSORS: You'll always need a pair of scissors. Keep a small pair in your knitting bag.

USE A FAVORITE PAINTING OR COLOR PHOTO FOR INSPIRATION.

PLAYING
with color

COPY COLORS FROM A VINTAGE QUILT.

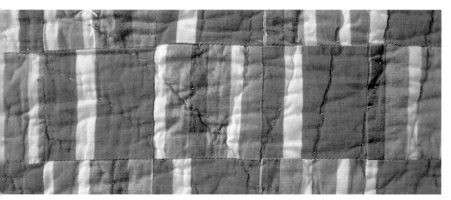

EXPLORE WALLPAPER AND FABRIC TO FIND NOVEL COLOR SCHEMES.

There are two types of knitters: Those who are into intense stitch patterns, like cables or lace, and those who are into working with color. I've always fallen in with the latter group. For me, knitting with color is like painting or taking a photograph. Sometimes I'm seeking to capture a certain mood or feeling, and at other moments I just like to see where the colors take me. Occasionally, I stick with one color family, but more often I challenge myself to introduce an 'ugly' color into the group or to knit with a handful of random colors. Having a limited amount of yarns on hand can be the beginning of a surprisingly beautiful project. My method of working with color is to start with what is in my stash and then buy a skein or three to flush it out.

Like most people, I have a palette that I prefer. Last year it was blues and greens. Now it's blood red, charcoal and cream. In order to keep my knitting interesting I challenge myself to embrace colors I despise. However, I am careful not to go with colors that I don't wear well or that I'm just not ready for. It's a fine line, but one thing I know for sure is that working with color in an unexpected way keeps me excited about my projects because I never know what will happen next!

PERUSE VINTAGE FASHION AND INTERIOR DESIGN MAGAZINES FOR COOL, RETRO PALETTES.

EVERYBODY KNOWS AN ADVENTUROUS DRESSER. WHAT CRAZY COLORS ARE YOUR LOCAL FASHION ICONS WORKING TODAY?

VARIOUS
+ SUNDRY

I WOULD GUESS THAT THE OVERWHELMING MAJORITY OF KNITTERS TODAY ARE NOT KNITTING BECAUSE THEY HAVE TO, BUT BECAUSE THEY WANT TO. I am sure this is even truer when it comes to creating non-wearable items. It takes a serious love for the craft of knitting to feel inspired to create something that isn't quite as necessary as a garment or an accessory. You just can't help but feel good whenever your eyes fall upon something that you have put your heart and soul into knitting just for the beauty of it. What's even better is that everyone who spends time in your space can partake in your pleasure when you play up your home décor with unique handknits.

Decoratives like table runners and afghans are great stash-busting projects. Try using the patterns in this chapter as a template for working with the yarn in your stash. Unlike garments, fit is not an issue. You can feel free to experiment with yarns that vary from the stated gauge. Fatter yarn will produce a bigger, heavier project, while finer yarns will give you something more lightweight and compact.

I love to give handcrafted gifts. Some of my favorite things to give are handknit washcloths paired with yummy soaps. It's a combination that appeals to all the senses! Like most knitters, I would never take the time to knit something like this for myself. However, I would be thrilled if a fellow knitter gifted me with a pair of these! This is definitely a present that both knitters and non-crafty people alike can enjoy. I chose hemp because it creates a sturdy fabric, and its nubby texture lends an exfoliating quality to these unique washcloths.

scrubs
{ EXFOLIATING WASHCLOTHS }

CONSTRUCTION NOTES

These washcloths are knitted in simple, textured rib patterns. Standard stitch patterns like these can be found in any basic stitch reference book. Be adventurous and try out a different stitch pattern, if you like.

SCRUB #1

MEASUREMENTS
10¼" X 10¼" (26CM X 26CM)

YARN
1 skein Hemp For Knitting
All Hemp 6
Pumpkin

NEEDLES
size US 4 (3.5mm) needles

If necessary, change needle size to obtain correct gauge.

GAUGE
24 sts and 30 rows = 4" (10cm) in pattern

SCRUB #2

MEASUREMENTS
11" X 11" (30CM X 30CM)

YARN
1 skein Hemp For Knitting
All Hemp 6
Classic Hemp

NEEDLES
size US 4 (3.5mm) needles

If necessary, change needle size to obtain correct gauge.

GAUGE
23 sts and 32 rows = 4" (10cm) in stitch pattern

SCRUB #1

With size US 4 (3.5mm) needles and Pumpkin hemp, CO 62 sts. Knit 4 rows.

BEGIN BROKEN RIB

ROWS 1–6: k3, * k2, p2; rep from * to last 3 sts, k3.

ROWS 7–12: k3, * p2, k2; rep from * to last 3 sts, k3.

Repeat Rows 1–12 until piece measures approx 10¼" (26cm), ending with Row 2.

Knit 4 rows. Bind off all sts and weave in ends.

SCRUB #2

With size US 4 (3.5mm) needles and classic hemp, CO 63 sts. Knit 4 rows.

BEGIN GARTER RIB

ROW 1: k1, * k1, p1; rep from * to last 2 sts, k2.

ROW 2: Knit.

Rep Rows 1–2 until piece measures approx 11" (30cm), ending with Row 2.

Knit 4 rows. Bind off all sts and weave in ends.

TIP

If you knit a pair of washcloths, you'll have enough yarn left over to crochet a border in a contrasting color. To create a border, work one row of single crochet around the edges of the washcloth using a size E crochet hook (see Glossary, page 120).

Those of us not fortunate enough to have had mothers and grandmothers engaged in needlework and other handcrafts are left with the wonderful task of making our own handmade memorables. Knitted items that get everyday use can be even more precious than heirloom quality pieces reserved for special occasions, because they serve as a constant reminder of the love and patience it took to knit them. Nothing cheers me up more than being surrounded by my handknit creations. This is the bath mat your Nana would have knit if your Nana were a knitter.

nana
{ BATH MAT }

CONSTRUCTION NOTES

At first glance, this bath mat looks like it's knit in plain old garter stitch. Look a little more closely, and you'll see that the knit-purl pattern actually creates a fabric with a corrugated look. The mat is worked with two pieces of yarn stranded together to create a thick, sturdy fabric.

MEASUREMENTS
20" X 32" (51CM X 81CM)

YARN
4 skeins Lion Brand Lion Cotton
 #144 Grape (MC)

1 skein Lion Brand Lion Cotton
 #210 Denim Swirl (CC)

NEEDLES AND HOOKS
size US 10½ (6.5mm) needles

If necessary, change needle size to obtain correct gauge.

size K crochet hook

GAUGE
Working with 2 strands held together, 14 sts and 20 rows = 4" (10cm) over stitch pattern

BATH MAT

With size US 10½ (6.5mm) needles and 2 strands of MC, CO 70 sts and knit 2 rows.

BEGIN STITCH PATTERN
ROW 1: k1, * k2, p2; rep from * to last st, k1.

ROW 2: k1, * p2, k2; rep from * to last st, k1.

Repeat Rows 1 and 2 until piece measures approximately 31½" (80cm), ending with row 2.

Knit 2 rows. Bind off all sts.

FINISHING
With 2 strands of CC and size K crochet hook, work 1 round of slip stitch around edges of bath mat, then 1 round of single crochet (see Glossary, page 120). Weave in all ends.

One of my favorite TV shows is *The Antiques Roadshow*. I was watching it one afternoon as I was finishing up Georgetown. I looked up from my knitting to glance at the screen, and I saw a woven textile that was almost identical to my project! I almost dropped my needles! The appraiser described it as "a historic Navaho blanket." This strange moment of synchronicity made me feel as though I had tapped into a collective creative consciousness where all design—past, present, and future—resides. Wouldn't it be fantastic if something you created to be used around the house survived to become a sought-after treasure 165 years from now?

georgetown
{ TABLE RUNNER }

CONSTRUCTION NOTES

Instead of knitting back and forth across the shorter width of this piece, you'll create extra-long stripes by knitting lengthwise. Switching between garter stitch and seed stitch lends texture to the table runner, and best of all, leaving long tails at each end when switching colors creates automatic fringe and keeps you from having to weave in ends.

MEASUREMENTS
64" X 8" (163CM X 20CM)

YARN
2 skeins Rowan Denim
    #225 *Nashville (A)*

3 skeins Rowan Denim
    #229 *Memphis (B)*

1 skein Rowan Denim
    #231 *Tennessee (C)*

2 skeins Rowan Denim
    #324 *Ecru (D)*

NEEDLES AND HOOKS
40" (100cm) size US 6 (4mm) circular needle

If necessary, change needle size to obtain correct gauge.

GAUGE
20 sts and 40 rows = 4" (10cm) in garter stitch

TABLE RUNNER

With 40" (102cm) size US 6 (4mm) circular needle and B, CO 289 sts.

note: At the end and beg of each row, leave a 6" (41cm) tail of yarn to create fringe. To secure each tail, tie it to the tail from the previous row using an overhand knot.

ROWS 1–6: Knit with B.

ROWS 7–9: Knit with A.

ROWS 10–11: Work in seed stitch with B.

ROWS 12–14: Knit with D.

ROWS 15–20: Work in seed stitch with A.

ROWS 21–25: Knit with C.

ROW 26: Knit with D.

ROWS 27–28: Knit with B.

ROWS 29–34: Knit with C.

ROWS 35–37: Knit with B.

ROWS 38–39: Work in seed stitch with A.

ROWS 40–42: Knit with B.

ROWS 43–48: Work in seed stitch with D.

ROWS 49–53: Knit with A.

ROW 54: Knit with C.

ROWS 55–56: Knit with D.

ROWS 57–62: Knit with B.

ROWS 63–65: Knit with C.

ROWS 66–67: Work in seed stitch with B.

ROWS 68–70: Knit with A.

ROWS 71–76: Work in seed stitch with B.

ROWS 77–81: Knit with D.

ROW 82: Knit with A.

ROWS 83–84: Knit with C.

ROWS 85–90: Knit with D.

Bind off all sts. There are no ends to weave in! All tails are now fringe.

TIP

The darker blue denim yarns are meant to fade like a well-worn pair of blue jeans. With use and washing, the darker blue shades might bleed onto lighter surrounding yarns. Try drycleaning if you want to keep your Georgetown looking crisp and new.

The first things I notice when I enter a room are the artwork and handcrafted objects. They tell me about the personality of the space and the people who live there. A rigid matchy-matchy decor with no room for mischief or surprise leaves me cold, while a playful mix of styles and eras can be immensely cheerful. One or two pieces like this hand-knit cushion add warmth to a room, transforming a space from rigid and unimaginative to unique and cozy.

havana
{ CUSHION COVER }

CONSTRUCTION NOTES

Each side of this pillow cover is a two-color square. The bottom of each square is a narrow strip turned on its side, and the remainder of the square is knitted from picked-up stitches along one edge of the narrow strip. One of the squares has a triangular flap made with simple decreases. The squares are seamed together and the top is left open for the flap to cover, secured by a simple button-and-loop closure.

MEASUREMENTS
16" X 16" (41CM X 41CM)

YARN
5 skeins Araucania Nature Cotton
  #8 light pink (MC)

2 skeins Araucania Nature Cotton
  #11 dark pink (CC)

NEEDLES
size US 13 (9mm) needles

If necessary, change needle size to obtain correct gauge.

NOTIONS
1 large rounded button or button with shank

GAUGE
Working with 2 strands held together, 10 sts and 20 rows = 4" (10cm) in garter stitch

SIDE A
With size US 13 (9mm) needles and MC, CO 14 sts. Work in garter stitch until piece measures approx 16" (41cm) from cast-on edge. Bind off all sts.

Turn so that garter ridges are vertical. With CC, pick up and knit 40 sts across top edge. Work in garter stitch until entire piece measures 16" (41cm). Bind off all sts.

SIDE B
Work Side B as for Side A until piece measures 16" (41cm).

NEXT ROW: k2tog, knit to last 2 sts, SSK.

ROW 2: Knit.

Rep Rows 1–2 until 2 sts rem. Bind off and make a small loop (for buttonhole) at the point of the fabric.

FINISHING
Sew side seams. Sew on button.

33

mod *on* mod
{ **AFGHAN** }

This blanket incorporates a lot of my favorite elements and ideas. I love repetitive patterns, especially when they are knit in different colors and sizes. The range of design possibilities is endless! Everyone expects an afghan to be knit with wool. But who says you can't choose a different fiber? Knitting this afghan with a textured cotton gives it a feel reminiscent of a vintage chenille bedspread. Mod On Mod works equally well adorning a sofa or spread across a bed.

CONSTRUCTION NOTES

This blanket is made up of 20 separate knitted squares seamed together into a large afghan. Four different intarsia motifs in complementary colors create an interesting effect.

MEASUREMENTS
42" X 65" (107CM X 165CM)

YARN
4 skeins Patagonia Nature Cotton
#203 *variegated light pink (A)*

4 skeins Patagonia Nautre Cotton
#209 *variegated tomato (B)*

4 skeins Araucania Nature Cotton
#4 *tangerine (C)*

3 skeins Araucania Nature Cotton
#16 *light pink (D)*

4 skeins Araucania Nature Cotton
#11 *fuchsia (E)*

NEEDLES
size US 9 (5.5mm) needles

If necessary, change needle size to obtain correct gauge.

GAUGE
15 sts and 22 rows = 4" (10cm) in stockinette stitch

AFGHAN

THERE ARE 4 SQUARE PATTERNS. THE BORDER COLOR IS THE MAIN COLOR (MC) AND THE CONTRASTING COLOR (CC) IS USED FOR THE SMALLER SQUARE. EACH SQUARE MEASURES 10½" X 13" (27CM X 33CM).

SQUARE 1 (MAKE 5)
With size US 9 (5.5mm) needles and MC, CO 39 sts.

ROWS 1–2: Knit with MC.

ROW 3 AND ALL ODD ROWS THROUGH 15: Knit.

ROW 4 AND ALL EVEN ROWS THROUGH 16: k2, p35, k2.

ROW 17 AND ALL ODD ROWS THROUGH 57: k7 with MC, knit 25 with CC, k7 with MC.

ROW 18 AND ALL EVEN ROWS THROUGH 58: k2 with MC, p5 with MC, p25 with CC, p5 with MC, k2 with MC.

ROW 59 AND ALL ODD ROWS THROUGH 71: Knit with MC.

ROW 60 AND ALL EVEN ROWS THROUGH 72: k2, p35, k2 with MC.

ROWS 73–74: Knit with MC.

Bind off all sts.

SQUARE 2 (MAKE 5)
With US 9 (5.5mm) needles and MC, CO 39 sts.

ROWS 1–2: Knit.

ROW 3 AND ALL ODD ROWS THROUGH 25: Knit.

ROW 4 AND ALL EVEN ROWS THROUGH 26: k2, p35, k2.

ROW 27 AND ALL ODD ROWS THROUGH 47: k13 with MC, k13 with CC, k13 with MC.

ROW 28 AND ALL EVEN ROWS THROUGH 48: k2 with MC, p11 with MC, p13 with CC, p11 with MC, k2 with MC.

ROW 49 AND ALL ODD ROWS THROUGH 71: Knit with MC.

ROW 50 AND ALL EVEN ROWS THROUGH 72: k2, p35, k2 with MC.

ROWS 73–74: Knit with MC.

Bind off all sts.

SQUARE 3 (MAKE 5)
With US 9 (5.5mm) needle and MC, CO 39 sts.

ROWS 1–2: Knit.

ROW 3 AND ALL ODD ROWS THROUGH 31: Knit.

ROW 4 AND ALL EVEN ROWS THROUGH 32: k2, p35, k2.

ROW 33 AND ALL ODD ROWS THROUGH 41: k16 with MC, k7 with CC, k16 with MC.

ROW 34 AND ALL EVEN ROWS THROUGH 42: k2 with MC, p14 with MC, p7 with CC, p14 with MC, k2 with MC.

ROW 43 AND ALL ODD ROWS THROUGH 71: Knit with MC.

ROW 44 AND ALL EVEN ROWS THROUGH 72: k2, p35, k2 with MC.

ROWS 73–74: Knit with MC.

Bind off all sts.

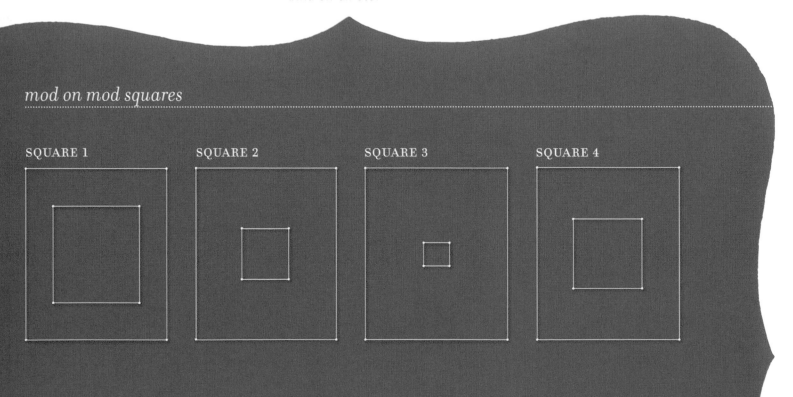

mod on mod squares

SQUARE 1   SQUARE 2   SQUARE 3   SQUARE 4

SQUARE 4 (MAKE 5)

With US 9 (5.5mm) needle and MC, CO 39 sts.

ROWS 1–2: Knit.

ROW 3 AND ALL ODD ROWS THROUGH 21: Knit.

ROW 4 AND ALL EVEN ROWS THROUGH 24: k2, p35, k2.

ROW 23 AND ALL ODD ROWS THROUGH 51: k10 with MC, k19 with CC, k10 with MC.

ROW 24 AND ALL EVEN ROWS THROUGH 52: k2 with MC, p8 with MC, p19 with CC, p8 with MC, k2 with MC.

ROW 53 AND ALL ODD ROWS THROUGH 71: Knit with MC.

ROW 54 AND ALL EVEN ROWS THROUGH 72: k2, p35, k2 with MC.

ROWS 73–74: Knit with MC.

Bind off all sts.

FINISHING

Arrange all of the squares on a flat surface, according to the diagram or as it pleases you. With a yarn needle and coordinating color of yarn, stitch squares together using mattress stitch. Weave in all ends.

TIP

Feel free to use this pattern as a template for your own unique arrangement of colors and squares. Please note that the yarn requirements listed are for Mod on Mod as designed. Yarn quantities may vary with a different arrangement.

NOTES: *switching colors*

At each color change, yarns must be wrapped around each other at the back of the work to prevent holes in the fabric. You may work with separate skeins, with yarn wound on bobbins, or with very long strands of yarn. Take time to untangle your strands every few rows.

mod on mod square layout

MC–E CC–D	MC–B CC–A	MC–A CC–E	MC–B CC–D
3	**4**	**2**	**1**
MC–A CC–C	MC–D CC–A	MC–B CC–C	MC–D CC–C
4	**3**	**1**	**2**
MC–C CC–B	MC–E CC–B	MC–C CC–E	MC–E CC–A
3	**2**	**4**	**1**
MC–B CC–D	MC–D CC–E	MC–A CC–C	MC–D CC–B
2	**1**	**3**	**4**
MC–A CC–B	MC–C CC–A	MC–E CC–A	MC–B CC–E
1	**2**	**4**	**3**

MC: MAIN COLOR   CC: CONTRAST COLOR

KEY

A Patagonia 203
Nature Cotton
variegated light pink

B Patagonia 209
Nature Cotton
variegated tomato

C Araucania
Nature Cotton 4
tangerine

D Araucania
Nature Cotton 16
light pink

E Araucania
Nature Cotton 11
fuchsia

HATS + SUCH

HATS AND SCARVES ARE THE BREAD AND BUTTER OF KNITTING.
EVERYBODY WANTS TO KNIT THEM, AND THERE IS NO SHORTAGE OF
birthdays, holidays and other gift-giving occasions on which they can be given to a
favorite pal or family member. They are a great portable project to toss into your bag
and knit on the bus or subway. Also, they are perfect when time or money is an issue
and you just can't commit to a bigger project like a sweater.

What I find really fantastic is that no two people wearing a hat or scarf knit from
the same pattern will wear it the same way. There are countless ways to wrap a scarf.
Similarly, some like their hats pulled down with the brim flipped back, while others
like to let them hang off the back of their heads. Everyone adds his or her own twist,
creating a completely fresh look.

When I see someone on the street wearing a handknit scarf and hat, I often won-
der what the person's relationship is to the knitter. Was the hat knit by a sweetheart?
Or a beloved Grandmother? Maybe it was knit by a best friend? Regardless of who
turned out these labors of love, you can be sure that the recipient feels special every
time he or she wears them!

sidetracked
{ MEN'S SCARF + HAT }

Nothing makes a project look more impressive than incorporating different colors and patterns in an unexpected way. Your friends will think you know your way around a skein or two when they see you sporting Sidetracked! What they don't know is that you don't need a lot of knitting experience to take on this super-easy project. These earthy colors with a zing of orange are great for a man, but this can also be an opportunity to play around and choose an entirely different palette.

CONSTRUCTION NOTES

With its ribbed brim and simple decreases for crown shaping, this classic hat is the perfect introduction for knitting on circular needles. The scarf is knitted lengthwise in very long rows, alternating between garter stitch and seed stitch to create an interesting texture that complements the variegated yarn.

MEASUREMENTS

HAT TO FIT SIZES	
SMALL	21" (53CM)
MEDIUM	22" (56CM)
LARGE	23" (59CM)

SCARF
6" X 56" (15CM X 142CM)

YARN
2 (2, 3) skeins Filatura di Crosa
127 Print
  #14 variegated off-white with browns (A)

1 skein Filatura di Crosa
127 Print
  #18 variegated black (B)

2 (2, 3) skeins Filatura di Crosa
127 Print
  #21 variegated tan and khaki (C)

NEEDLES
16" (40cm) size US 9 (5.5mm) circular needle

32"–40" (80cm-100cm) size US 9 (5.5mm) circular needle

size US 9 (5.5mm) dpn

If necessary, change needle size to obtain correct gauge.

GAUGE
16 sts and 26 rows = 4" (10cm) in stockinette stitch

45

NOTES: *seed stitch*

Seed stitch is worked by knitting all purl stitches and purling all knit stitches. Here's how it works:

FOR AN ODD NUMBER OF STITCHES

ROW 1: * k1, p1; rep from * until last st, k1.

Rep Row 1.

FOR AN EVEN NUMBER OF STITCHES

ROW 1: * k1, p1; rep from * until end of row.

ROW 2: * p1, k1; rep from * until end of row.

Rep Rows 1 and 2.

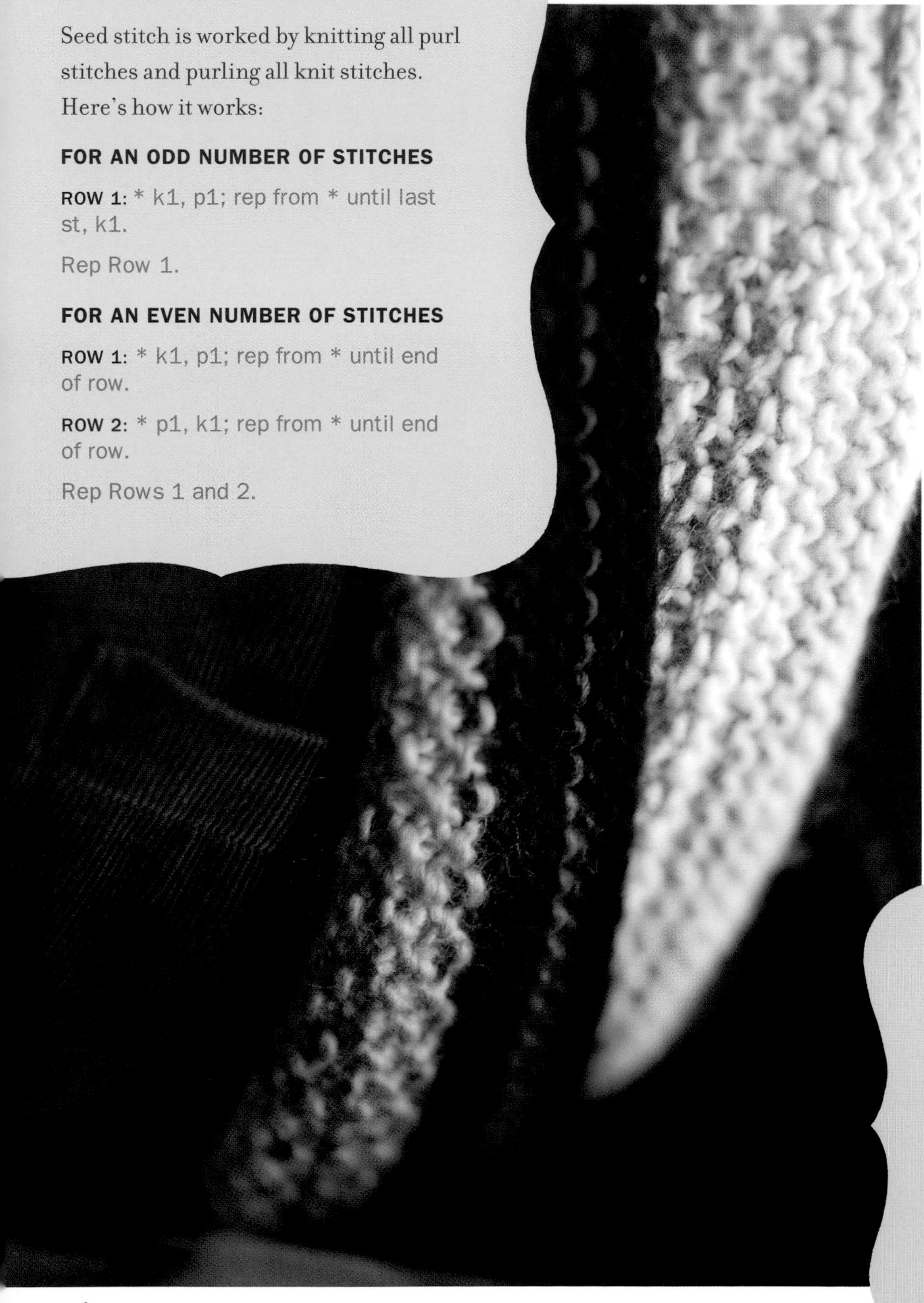

SCARF

With size US 9 (5.5mm) 32"–40" (80cm–100cm) circular needle and A, cast on 201 sts.

Work in garter stitch for 1¼" (3cm), then work in seed stitch for 1¼" (3cm). Cont to alternate between garter and seed stitch in 1¼" (3cm) increments. At the same time, when work measures 2½" (6cm) from cast-on edge, cut yarn and join in C. Work in the established pattern with C until work measures 4¾" (12cm). Cut yarn and join in B and cont in established pattern until work measures 6¼" (16cm) from cast-on edge.

Bind off all sts and weave in ends.

NOTES: *k2tog*

Knitting two stitches together as one (k2tog) is a simple way to decrease the number of stitches in a row. Simply slip your right hand needle through the first two stitches on the left hand needle from front to back, as for a regular knit stitch. Knit the two stitches as one, creating one less stitch.

HAT

With size US 9 (5.5mm) 16" (41cm) circular needle, CO 84 (88, 92) sts with B. Join sts for working in the round, taking care not to twist sts. Work in k2, p2 rib for 3 rnds.

RNDS 4–7: Cont in k2, p2 rib with C.

RNDS 8–12: Cont in k2, p2 rib with A.

RNDS 13–15: Knit with B.

RNDS 16–17: Knit with C.

Repeat Rnds 13–17 twice.

RNDS 28–29: Knit with A.

RNDS 30–31: Knit with B.

RNDS 32–34: Knit with C.

RNDS 35–36: Knit with A.

Repeat Rnds 32–36 for the remainder of the hat. Work straight until hat measures 7" (18cm) from cast-on edge.

CROWN SHAPING

RND 1:
  SMALL: Knit (84 sts).
  MEDIUM: * k20, k2tog; rep from * to end (84 sts).
  LARGE: * k9, k2tog; rep from * to last 4 sts, k4 (84 sts).

RND 2: * k10, k2tog; rep from * to end (77 sts).

RND 3: *k9, k2tog; rep from * to end (70 sts).

RND 4: * k8, k2tog; rep from * to end (63 sts).

RND 5: * k7, k2tog; rep from * to end (56 sts).

RND 6: * k6, k2tog; rep from * to end (49 sts).

RND 7: * k5, k2tog; rep from * to end (42 sts).

RND 8: * k4, k2tog; rep from * to end (35 sts).

RND 9: * k3, k2tog; rep from * to end (28 sts).

RND 10: * k2tog; rep from * to end (14 sts).

Cut yarn, leaving an 8" (20cm) tail. Thread tail through rem sts and weave in firmly on wrong side of hat. Weave in all rem tails.

NOTES: *working in the round*

If this is your first in-the-round project, you may not believe this: knitting in the round is easier than knitting on straight needles. Here's why: To produce a beautiful and quick stockinette stitch, you only have to knit. No purling! Seriously.

Before you begin, make sure that your circular needles are a bit shorter than the diameter of your project. For instance, to make the Sidetracked hat, you need needles that are 16" (40cm). Simply cast on the requisite number of stitches just as on straight needles. Hold the needle with the tail dangling from it in your left hand. Push the stitches to the end of the needle. Hold the needle with the working yarn in your right hand, pushing the first stitches to the end of that needle. Insert the tip of the right needle into the first stitch on the left needle from front to back. Wrap the working yarn around the right needle and knit your first stitch. Voilá, you're connected! Knit every round, being careful not to twist your stitches.

The illustration at right is for working in the round using double-pointed needles. You generally need to switch to dpns at the crown of a hat, when the stitches get too tight. See the Glossary, page 120, for information on casting on with dpns.

47

tami

{ RIBBED SCARF + HAT }

When I was a little girl, I was all about accessories. No winter outfit was complete without a matching hat and scarf. Now that I am a much bigger girl, I still find this essential cold weather set really sweet! I love the sugary raspberry color, but you can also choose a guy-friendly shade and knit it up for your style-conscious beau! With a matching hat and scarf set, you might just look forward to that first cold winter's day.

CONSTRUCTION NOTES

This project is an easy introduction to working with a stitch pattern and learning advanced techniques, such as picking up stitches. The scarf is knit in a simple broken rib. To make the hat, you'll first knit the brim in a long strip. Then the ends of the brim are sewn together to create a circle. The rest of the hat is knitted on circular needles by picking up stitches from the brim.

MEASUREMENTS

HAT TO FIT SIZES

SMALL	21" (53CM)
MEDIUM	22" (56CM)
LARGE	23" (58CM)

SCARF

APPROX 6½" X 72" (17CM X 183CM)

YARN

6 (6, 7) skeins Filatura di Crosa 127 Print

#37 variegated pink

NEEDLES

size US 8 (5mm) needles

16" (40cm) size US 8 (5mm) circular needle

size US 8 (5mm) dpn

If necessary, change needle size to obtain correct gauge.

GAUGE

16 sts and 26 rows = 4" (10cm) in stockinette stitch

SCARF

With yarn and US 8 (5mm) needles, CO 35 sts. *k2, p2; rep from * to last 3 sts, k2, p1. Repeat this row until your scarf measures 72" (183cm). Bind off all sts and weave in ends.

HAT

BRIM

With size US 8 (5mm) circular needle, CO 11 (11, 11) sts. * k2, p2; rep from * to last 3 sts, k2, p1. Rep this row until piece measures 21¼ (22¼, 23¼)" (54 [57, 59]cm). Bind off all sts. Sew up back seam.

MAIN SECTION

With size US 8 (5mm) circular needle, pick up and k84 (88, 92) sts around top of brim. Join yarn for working in the round. Purl 1 rnd. Knit next and all foll rnds. Cont straight in stockinette until hat measures 7" (18cm) from bottom edge of brim.

CROWN SHAPING

RND 1: Dec 3 (0, 2) sts evenly spaced across rnd (81 [88, 90] sts).

RND 2: * k7 (9, 8), k2tog; rep from * to end (72 [80, 81] sts).

RND 3: * k6 (8, 7), k2tog; rep from * to end (63 [72, 72] sts).

RND 4: * k5 (7, 6), k2tog; rep from * to end (54 [64, 63] sts).

RND 5: * k4 (6, 5), k2tog; rep from * to end (45 [56, 54] sts).

RND 6: * k3 (5, 4), k2tog; rep from * to end (36 [48, 45] sts).

RND 7: * k2 (4, 3), k2tog; rep from * to end (27 [40, 36] sts).

RND 8: * k1 (3, 2), k2tog; rep from * to end (18 [32, 27] sts).

RND 9:
SMALL: * k2tog; rep from * to end (9 sts).
MEDIUM: * k2, k2tog; rep from * to end (24 sts).
LARGE: * k1, k2tog; rep from * to end (18 sts)

RND 10:
MEDIUM: * k1, k2tog; rep from * to end (16 sts).
LARGE: * k2tog; rep from * to end (9 sts).

RND 11 (SIZE MED ONLY): * k2tog; rep from * to end (8 sts).

Cut yarn, leaving an 8" (20cm) tail. Use a yarn needle to pull the tail through rem sts on knitting needles. Tighten the tail to pull sts together and then weave the end in firmly on wrong side of hat. Weave in all other ends.

NOTES: *picking up stitches*

For the Tami Hat, you'll be picking up stitches around the top of the brim. Simply insert the tip of one needle through the edge of the fabric from front to back. Leaving about a 3"–4" (8cm–10cm) tail, wrap yarn around the needle as you would for a regular knit stitch. Bring the yarn through the stitch, creating a loop on your needle. This loop is the first picked-up stitch. Continue to pick up the number of stitches required, making sure to space them evenly.

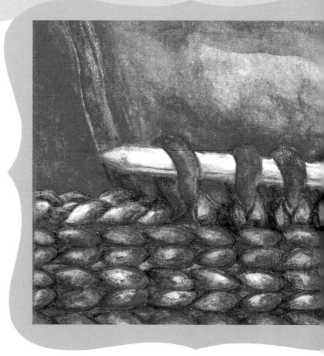

austin
{ ARMWARMERS }

A couple of years ago I moved from the northeast to the south. The change in climate has been a huge adjustment for me. When I expect it to be cold, it's hot. When I expect it to be hot, it's even hotter. Abundant air conditioning in the summertime makes indoor temperatures just as extreme. Lightweight yarn makes these armwarmers perfect to wear with a t-shirt and a light jacket on a changeable winter day or to wear indoors at the height of air-conditioned summer. Whether you want to get warm or look cool, these armwarmers are perfect!

CONSTRUCTION NOTES

These armwarmers are really just long, skinny tubes with ribbing at either end. They are a great warm-up for knitting more complicated in-the-round projects, like socks. Knitting the first few rounds takes concentration, but after an inch or two, it's pretty effortless.

MEASUREMENTS
PATTERN AS GIVEN IS 17" (43CM) IN LENGTH, 6" (16CM) AROUND WRIST, AND 10" (25CM) AROUND UPPER ARM

YARN
1 skein Lorna's Laces Shepherd Sport
 #38 Mixed Berry (MC)

1 skein Lorna's Laces Shepherd Sport
 #45 Cranberry (CC)

NEEDLES
size US 3 (3.25mm) double-pointed needles (dpn)

size US 2 (2.75mm) dpn (optional)

If necessary, change needle size to obtain correct gauge.

GAUGE
28 sts and 36 rows = 4" (10cm) in slightly stretched k2, p2 rib on size 3 (3.25mm) needles

ARMWARMERS

WRIST CUFF

CO 44 sts with CC and size US 3 (3.25mm) dpn. Divide sts evenly over four needles and join, taking care not to twist sts. You may pm to mark beg of rnd, or use the tail from the cast on as a marker. Work in k2, p2 rib for 6" (15cm).

MIDSECTION

At beg of next rnd, switch to MC and reverse rib by working in p2, k2 rib. Work straight for 6 rnds.

BEGIN INCREASES

Inc 1 st at beg and end of next rnd and every foll seventh rnd 11 times (68 sts), working inc into pattern. At the same time, when piece measures 14" (36cm) from cast-on edge, change to CC and reverse rib by working in k2, p2 rib.

UPPER ARM CUFF

When inc are complete, cont straight until armwarmer measures 17" (43cm) from cast-on edge. Bind off all sts and weave in ends. If desired, you may work the final ½" (1cm) of the upper arm cuff with size US 2 (2.75mm) dpn to make the ribbing a little tighter.

NOTES: *personalizing your fit*

If you'd like to tailor your armwarmers to fit the exact dimensions of your arms, follow these simple calculations.

NUMBER OF STITCHES TO CAST ON FOR WRIST

Circumference around wrist bone + ½" (1cm) = A

Number of sts per inch x A = B

Round this sum up so it is divisible by 4.

B IS THE NUMBER OF STITCHES TO CAST ON.

NUMBER OF STITCHES TO ACCOMMODATE UPPER ARM

Circumference of elbow (with arm outstretched) + ½" (1cm) = C

Number of stitches per inch x C = D

Round this sum up so it is divisible by 4.

D IS THE NUMBER OF STS NEEDED TO ACCOMMODATE UPPER ARM.

NUMBER OF INCREASE ROUNDS TO BE WORKED

D – B / 2 = E

E IS THE NUMBER OF INCREASE ROUNDS TO BE WORKED.

Remember, you may need additional yarn if your armwarmers are larger than the size given in the pattern.

NOTES: *casting on with double-pointed needles*

If one of your double-pointed needles can accommodate the full number of stitches, cast all of the stitches onto one needle. If your needles are shorter, you may opt to cast all of the stitches onto one longer straight needle. Once all of the stitches have been cast on, divide them evenly between four of the dpn. To divide the stitches, hold the needle with the cast-on stitches in your left hand, as if to knit. Using a dpn, insert the tip of the needle into the first stitch as if to purl. Slip the stitch to the right-hand needle. Continue to slip stitches as if to purl until there are 11 stitches on each of four needles. The remaining dpn is for knitting. See page 47 for an illustration of connecting stitches for working in the round with double-pointed needles.

When I design, the project idea usually comes before the yarn selection. However, with Clutched, the yarn inspired the project. One hundred percent of the sales of Peace Fleece Worsted, in the color Baghdad Blue, is donated to Neve Shalom/Wahat al Salam, a village in Israel established jointly by Jews and Palestinian Arabs of Israeli citizenship who are engaged in educational work for peace, equality and understanding between the two peoples.

This quick project can be knit up within a couple of days, making it a great gift or the perfect way to scratch your itch for a fast knitting fix!

clutched
{ HANDBAG }

CONSTRUCTION NOTES

Knitted as one large rectangular piece of fabric, this purse requires only minimal assembly. Once knitted, the bottom of the rectangle is folded up and seamed to the purse opening. The remainder of the rectangle folds over the top to become a flap. Worked with two strands of yarn held together, this textured clutch is as functional as it is pretty.

MEASUREMENTS
12" (30CM) WIDE BY 6" (15CM) TALL WITH FLAP CLOSED

YARN
2 skeins Peace Fleece Worsted
Baghdad Blue

NEEDLES
size US 11 (8mm) needles

If necessary, change needle size to obtain correct gauge.

NOTIONS
two ¾–1" (2cm–2.5cm) buttons

GAUGE
Working with 2 strands of yarn held together, 11 sts and 20 rows = 4" (10cm) in stitch pattern

CLUTCH

With size US 11 (8mm) needles and 2 strands of yarn, CO 33 sts.

ROW 1: * k1, p1; repeat from * to last st, k1.

Repeat Row 1 until piece measures 13" (33cm), ending with a WS row.

FLAP
NEXT ROW: k1, p1, k29, p1, k1.

ROW 2: k1, p1, k1, p27, k1, p1, k1.

Repeat these 2 rows 5 more times.

BUTTONHOLE ROWS
NEXT ROW: k1, p1, k3, yo, k2tog, k19, k2tog, yo, k3, p1, k1.

ROW 2: * k1, p1; rep to last st, k1.

Repeat Row 2 five more times.

Bind off all sts in pattern.

FINISHING
Fold up bottom of bag to approx 6" (15cm). Sew side seams. Sew on buttons to align with buttonholes.

Do not block!

TIP
If you want a super-stiff fabric, don't block!

manta ray
{ SHAWL }

Whether you are cruising the flea market on a Saturday morning or meeting up with friends for a special celebration, Manta Ray is definitely the shawl to be seen in! Its dramatic look raises the bar on a casual outfit, or it can be the pièce de résistance of an elegant evening ensemble. Open stitchwork makes this versatile wrap look light and airy, but it's decptively warm. Wear it any way you like—double it up corner-to-corner, fold it in half lengthways, or just wear it unfurled.

CONSTRUCTION NOTES

This shawl is worked from corner to corner, beginning with just three stitches and increasing two stitches in the center until the full number of stitches is acheived. Continue knitting for a longer and wider shawl, or stop at your desired length if you prefer your Manta Ray short and sweet.

MEASUREMENTS
50" X 50" (127CM X 127CM)

YARN
1 skein Lorna's Laces Heaven
   #70 Vera

NEEDLES
size US 8 (5mm) circular needle,
32" (80cm) or longer

If necessary, change needle size to obtain correct gauge.

GAUGE
16 sts and 32 rows = 4" (10cm) in garter stitch

61

SHAWL

With size US 8 (5mm) 32" (81cm) circular needle, CO 3 sts.

ROW 1 AND ALL ODD ROWS: Knit.

ROW 2: Inc 1, k1, inc 1.

ROW 4: k2, yo, k1, yo, k2.

ROW 6: k2, yo, k3, yo, k2.

ROW 8: k3, yo, k3, yo, k3.

ROW 10: k4, yo, k3, yo, k4.

ROW 12: k3, yo, k2tog, yo, pm, k3, pm, yo, k2tog, yo, k3.

ROW 14: k3, yo, k2tog, knit to first marker, yo, slip marker, k3, slip marker, yo. Knit to last 5 sts, k2tog, yo, k3.

ROW 15: Knit.

Rep Rows 14 and 15 until length measures 50" (127cm).

Bind off all sts loosely and weave in ends.

TIP

Fold the collar back and secure the front with a brooch for a sophisticated look!

NOTES: *increases*

When you come to a yarn over in the pattern, simply wrap the working yarn around the right-hand needle and continue knitting as usual. On the following row, the wrapped yarn is treated just like a regular stitch.

There are lots of different ways to increase the number of stitches in a given row. If the pattern simply says inc 1, you choose the method of increasing that works best for you. An easy way to increase is to knit one in the front and back of a stitch (k1fb). To make this type of increase, simply insert your right hand needle into the next stitch on the left-hand needle and knit the stitch, but keep the stitch on the left-hand needle instead of sliding it off. Then bring your right-hand needle around to the back, knit into the back loop of the same stitch, and slip it off the needle. See the Glossary on page 121 for more increase methods.

copperhead
{ SCARF }

I like exaggerated shapes, so when I stumbled upon this medallion cable I knew I needed to blow it up and make it even bigger! The raised cable set against a narrow background gives the appearance of a snake in motion. Hence, the name Copperhead. It can be dressed up as an elegant evening wear accessory or dressed down with corduroys and a denim jacket. Either way, it will look dangerously chic!

CONSTRUCTION NOTES

The pointed ends of this scarf are created by simple increases and decreases. At first glance, Copperhead may seem more complicated than the other scarves in this chapter. The length of the pattern may seem daunting, but if you have a row counter handy, you'll find it easy to stay on track.

MEASUREMENTS
5½" X 78" (14CM X 198CM)
AFTER BLOCKING

YARN
2 skeins Lorna's Laces Lion & Lamb
   #102 Mineshaft

NEEDLES
size US 8 (5mm) needles

If necessary, change needle size to obtain correct gauge.

two cable needles

NOTIONS
row counter

GAUGE
18 sts and 24 rows = 4" (10cm) in stockinette stitch

SCARF

With size US 8 (5mm) needles,
CO 3 sts.

BEGIN INCREASES

ROW 1: k1, p1, k1.

ROW 2: p1, k1, p1.

ROW 3: Cont in seed st, inc 1 st at each end, working inc into pattern (5 sts).

ROWS 4–5: Work in seed st.

ROW 6: Cont in seed st, inc 1 st at each end, working inc into pattern (7 sts).

ROWS 7–8: Work in seed st.

ROW 9: Cont in seed st, inc 1 st at each end, working inc into pattern (9 sts).

ROWS 10–11: Work in seed st.

ROW 12: Cont in seed st, inc 1 st at each end, working inc into pattern (11 sts).

ROWS 13–14: Work in seed st.

ROW 15: Cont in seed st, inc 1 st at each end, working inc into pattern (13 sts).

ROW 16: (k1, p1) twice, k1, p3, (k1, p1) twice, k1.

ROW 17: (k1, p1) twice, k5, (p1, k1) twice.

ROW 18: (k1, p1) twice, k1, inc 1, p3, inc 1, (k1, p1) twice, k1 (15 sts).

ROW 19: (k1, p1) twice, k7, (p1, k1) twice.

ROW 20: (k1, p1) twice, k1, p5, (k1, p1) twice, k1.

ROW 21: (k1, p1) twice, k1, inc 1, k5, inc 1, (k1 p1) twice, k1 (17 sts).

ROW 22: (k1, p1) twice, k1, p7, (k1, p1) twice, k1.

ROW 23: (k1, p1) twice, k9, (p1, k1) twice.

ROW 24: (k1, p1) twice, k1, inc 1, p7, inc 1, (k1, p1) twice, k1 (19 sts).

ROW 25: (k1, p1) twice, k11, (p1, k1) twice.

ROW 26: (k1, p1) twice, k1, p9, (k1, p1) twice, k1.

ROW 27: (k1, p1) twice, k1, inc 1, k9, inc 1, (k1, p1) twice, k1 (21 sts).

ROW 28: (k1, p1) twice, k1, p11, (k1, p1) twice, k1.

ROW 29: (k1, p1) twice, k13, (p1, k1) twice.

ROW 30: (k1, p1) twice, k1, inc 1, p11, inc 1, (k1, p1) twice, k1 (23 sts).

ROW 31: (k1, p1) twice, k15, (p1, k1) twice.

ROW 32: (k1, p1) twice, k1, p13, (k1, p1) twice, k1.

ROW 33: (k1, p1) twice, k1, inc 1, k13, inc 1, (k1, p1) twice, k1 (25 sts).

ROW 34: (k1, p1) twice, k1, p15, (k1, p1) twice, k1.

ROW 35: (k1, p1) twice, k17, (p1, k1) twice.

ROW 36: (k1, p1) twice, k1, inc 1, p15, inc 1, (k1, p1) twice, k1 (27 sts).

ROW 37: (k1, p1) twice, k19, (p1, k1) twice.

ROW 38: (k1, p1) twice, k1, p17, (k1, p1) twice, k1.

ROW 39: (k1, p1) twice, k1, inc 1, k17, inc 1, (k1, p1) twice, k1 (29 sts).

ROW 40: (k1, p1) twice, k1, p19, (k1, p1) twice, k1.

ROW 41: (k1, p1) twice, k21, (p1, k1) twice.

ROW 42: (k1, p1) twice, k1, inc 1, p19, inc 1, (k1, p1) twice, k1 (31 sts).

ROW 43: (k1, p1) twice, k23, (p1, k1) twice.

BEGIN CABLE PATTERN

ROW 1: (k1, p1) twice, k1, p3, slip (sl) 5 sts to cn and hold at back of work, sl 5 sts to cn and hold at front of work, k5 from left-hand needle, k5 from left-hand needle, k5 from front cn, p3, (k1, p1) twice, k1.

ROW 2: (k1, p1) twice, k1, inc 1, k2, p17, k2, inc 1, (k1, p1) twice, k1 (33 sts).

ROW 3: (k1, p1) twice, k1, p4, k15, p4, (k1, p1) twice, k1.

ROW 4: (k1, p1) twice, k5, p15, k5, (p1, k1) twice.

ROW 5: (k1, p1) twice, k1, inc 1, p3, k17, p3, inc 1, (k1, p1) twice, k1 (35 sts).

ROW 6: (k1, p1) twice, k6, p15, k6, (p1, k1) twice.

ROW 7: (k1, p1) twice, k1, p5, k15, p5, (k1, p1) twice, k1.

ROW 8: (k1 p1) twice, k1, inc 1, k4, p17, k4, inc 1, (k1, p1) twice, k1 (37 sts).

ROW 9: (k1, p1) twice, k1, p6, k15, p6, (k1, p1) twice, k1.

ROW 10: (k1, p1) twice, k7, p15, k7, (p1, k1) twice.

ODD ROWS 11–23: Rep Row 9.

EVEN ROWS 12–24: Rep Row 10.

ROW 25: (k1, p1) twice, k1, p6, sl 5 sts to cn and hold at back of work, sl 5 sts to cn and hold at front of work, k5 from left hand needle, k5 from front cn, k5 from back cn, p6, (k1, p1) twice, k1.

EVEN ROWS 26–48: Rep Row 10.

ODD ROWS 27–47: Rep Row 9.

ROW 49: (k1, p1) twice, k1, p6, sl 5 sts to cn and hold at back of work, sl 5 sts to cn and hold at front of work, k5 from left-hand needle, k5 from front cn, k5 from back cn, p6, (k1, p1) twice, k1.

Rep Rows 26–49 13 more times.

BEGIN SCARF TIP

ODD ROWS 1–15: (k1, p1) twice, k7, p15, k7, (p1, k1) twice.

EVEN ROWS 2–16: (k1, p1) twice, k1, p6, k15, p6, (k1, p1) twice, k1.

ROW 17: (k1, p1) twice, k5, k2tog, p15, k2tog, k5, (p1, k1) twice (35 sts).

ROW 18: (k1, p1) twice, k1, p5, k15, p5, (k1, p1) twice, k1.

ROW 19: (k1, p1) twice, k6, p15, k6, (p1, k1) twice.

ROW 20: (k1, p1) twice, k1, p3, p2tog, k15, p2tog, p3, (k1, p1) twice, k1 (33 sts).

ROW 21: (k1, p1) twice, k5, p15, k5, (p1, k1) twice.

ROW 22: (k1, p1) twice, k1, p4, k15, p4, (k1, p1) twice, k1.

ROW 23: (k1, p1) twice, k3, k2tog, p15, k2tog, k3, (p1, k1) twice (31 sts).

ROW 24: (k1, p1) twice, k1, p3, sl 5 sts to cn and hold at back of work, sl 5 sts to cn and hold at front of work, k5 from left-hand needle, k5 from front cn, k5 from back cn, p3, (k1, p1) twice, k1.

DECREASE TO END SCARF

ROW 1: (k1, p1) twice, k23, (p1, k1) twice.

ROW 2: (k1, p1) twice, k1, p2tog, p17, p2tog, (k1, p1) twice, k1 (29 sts).

ROW 3: (k1, p1) twice, k21, (p1, k1) twice.

ROW 4: (k1, p1) twice, k1, p19, (k1, p1) twice, k1.

ROW 5: (k1, p1) twice, k1, k2tog, k15, k2tog, (k1, p1) twice, k1 (27 sts).

ROW 6: (k1, p1) twice, k1, p17, (k1, p1) twice, k1.

ROW 7: (k1, p1) twice, k19, (p1, k1) twice.

ROW 8: (k1, p1) twice, k1, p2tog, p13, p2tog, (k1, p1) twice, k1 (25 sts).

ROW 9: (k1, p1) twice, k17, (p1, k1) twice.

ROW 10: (k1, p1) twice, k1, p15, (k1, p1) twice, k1.

ROW 11: (k1, p1) twice, k1, k2tog, k11, k2tog, (k1, p1) twice, k1 (23 sts).

ROW 12: (k1, p1) twice, k1, p13, (k1, p1) twice, k1.

ROW 13: (k1, p1) twice, k15, (p1, k1) twice.

ROW 14: (k1, p1) twice, k1, p2tog, p9, p2tog, (k1, p1) twice, k1 (21 sts).

ROW 15: (k1, p1) twice, k13, (p1, k1) twice.

ROW 16: (k1, p1) twice, k1, p11, (k1, p1) twice, k1.

ROW 17: (k1, p1) twice, k1, k2tog, k7, k2tog, (k1, p1) twice, k1 (19 sts).

ROW 18: (k1, p1) twice, k1, p9, (k1, p1) twice, k1.

ROW 19: (k1, p1) twice, k11, (p1, k1) twice.

ROW 20: (k1, p1) twice, k1, p2tog, p5, p2tog, (k1, p1) twice, k1 (17 sts).

ROW 21: (k1, p1) twice, k9, (p1, k1) twice.

ROW 22: (k1, p1) twice, k1, p7, (k1, p1) twice, k1.

ROW 23: (k1, p1) twice, k1, k2tog, k3, k2tog, (k1, p1) twice, k1 (15 sts).

ROW 24: (k1, p1) twice, k1, p5, (k1, p1) twice, k1.

ROW 25: (k1, p1) twice, k7, (p1, k1) twice.

ROW 26: (k1, p1) twice, k1, p2tog, p1, p2tog, (k1, p1) twice, k1 (13 sts).

ROW 27: (k1, p1) twice, k5, (p1, k1) twice.

ROW 28: (k1, p1) twice, k1, p3, (k1, p1) twice, k1.

ROW 29: (k1, p1) twice, k2tog, p1, k2tog, (p1, k1) twice (11 sts).

ROWS 30–31: Work in seed st.

ROW 32: Cont in seed st, dec 1 st at each end, working dec into pattern (9 sts).

ROWS 33–34: Work in seed st.

ROW 35: Cont in seed st, dec 1 st at each end, working dec into pattern (7 sts).

ROWS 36–37: Work in seed st.

ROW 38: Cont in seed st, dec 1 st at each end, working dec into pattern (5 sts).

ROWS 39–40: Work in seed st.

ROW 41: Cont in seed st, dec 1 st at each end, working dec into pattern (3 sts).

ROWS 42–43: Work in seed st.

Bind off rem 3 sts. Weave in all ends.

TIP
Copperhead should be wet-blocked to prevent the edges from rolling.

NOTES: *cables*

Although cables may seem difficult, they're really quite simple. To create a cable, slip (sl) the number of stitches indicated in the pattern onto a cable needle (cn) and hold the cable needle at the front or back of the work, as directed. Then simply ignore the cable needle and knit the number of stitches indicated in the pattern from the left-hand needle. Rejoin the stitches on the cable needle to the main stitches by knitting them off of the cable needle. Holding the cable needle to the front or back of your work determines the way the cable will twist.

The cable in this scarf is fatter than in most other cables. The extra width of the cables is created by using two cable needles at once instead of just one.

TIP

Copperhead is shown here with the wrong side facing front. Scarves are famous for flipping from one side to the other, and Copperhead looks fabulous either way.

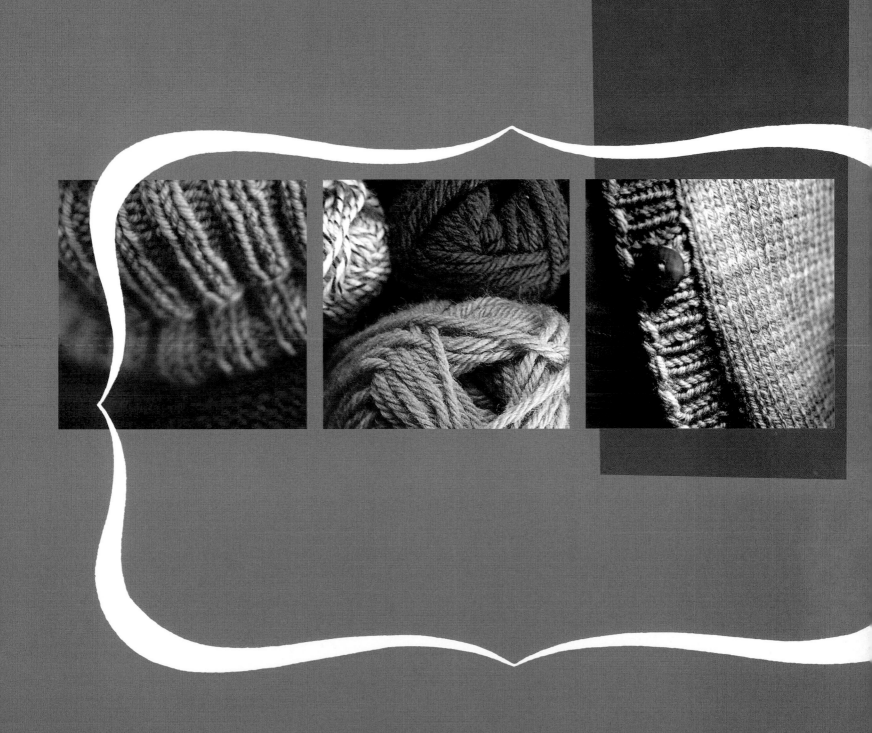

SWEATERS, VESTS
+ TANKS

I WEAR MY HANDKNIT GARMENTS LIKE SPIRITUAL ARMOR. THE COUNTLESS HOURS AND LOVING ATTENTION THAT GO INTO KNITTING A SWEATER create an energetic force field that protects me when I feel vulnerable and lifts my spirits when I feel down. Only those who have knit for themselves can understand the very special feeling you get when you wear something that has been created by your own hands.

Never underestimate the magical power of knitting! For ages men and women all over the world have been consciously knitting intentions into their creations. As you knit a child's sweater you might wish that he or she always be protected, while a lover's garment may be knit with the desire that your beloved remain faithful and true. A shawl for an elderly relative may be imbued with blessings for good health. No matter what your intention may be, the sweaters that you knit will bear the unique imprint of your energy, workmanship and love!

sloane
{ SWEATER VEST }

Sometimes you need a little knitted something to add personality to your outfit. When a scarf is not enough and a sweater is too much, a vest is perfect! Wear it with a button-down shirt and your favorite jeans for a look that is both cool and classic. Or, if you are feeling feisty, pair it with wool shorts and boots for a bolder look. Not only is Sloane stylish, she's also quick to knit. If you are looking for a fast and easy addition to your wardrobe, this project is for you. Everybody needs a little vest!

CONSTRUCTION NOTES

The front and back of this simple vest are knit separately and then seamed together. Simple shoulder shaping and no sleeves make this a great first sweater project.

MEASUREMENTS

TO FIT BUST	
X-SMALL	32" (81CM)
SMALL	34" (86CM)
MEDIUM	36" (91CM)
LARGE	38" (97CM)
X-LARGE	40" (102CM)

YARN

4 (4, 5, 5, 6) skeins Rowan Ribbon Twist
#115, Rapid

NEEDLES

size US 17 (12mm) 29" (74cm) circular needle

If necessary, change needle size to obtain correct gauge.

GAUGE

8 sts and 10 rows = 4" (10cm) in stockinette stitch

BACK

With size US 17 (12mm) needle, CO 32 (34, 36, 38, 40) sts. Work in k1, p1 rib for 12 rows.

NEXT ROW (RS): k16 (17, 18, 19, 20), inc 1, knit to end (33 [35, 37, 39, 41] sts). Cont straight in stockinette stitch until work measures 12¾ (12¾, 13¼, 13¼, 13¾)" (32 [32, 34, 34, 35]cm) from cast-on edge.

ARMHOLE SHAPING

Bind off 2 sts at beg of next 2 rows. Dec 1 st at each end of next row and every foll row 0 (0, 1, 1, 2) times (27 [29, 29, 31, 31] sts). Cont straight in stockinette stitch until armholes measure 7 (7½, 8, 8½, 8½)" (19 [19, 20, 22, 22]cm), ending with a WS row.

SHOULDER SHAPING

Bind off 2 sts at beg of next 2 rows. Bind off 2 sts, k1, turn. Bind off rem sts. Rejoin yarn and bind off center 15 (17, 17, 19, 19) sts, knit to end.

Complete rem shoulder to match first side, reversing shaping.

FRONT

Cast on and work ribbing as for back. Cont in stockinette stitch on 32 (34, 36, 38, 40) sts until work measures 12¼ (12¼, 12¾, 12¾, 13¼)" (31 [31, 33, 33, 34]cm) from cast-on edge.

NECK AND ARMHOLE SHAPING

NEXT ROW: k16 (17, 18, 19, 20), place rem sts on holder, turn. Dec 1 st at neck edge of next and every foll third row 4 (5, 5, 4, 4) times, then every foll alt row 2 (2, 2, 4, 4) times. Cont straight, if necessary, until armhole measures 7 (7½, 8, 8½, 8½)" (19 [19, 20, 22, 22]cm).

At the same time, after first neck dec, begin armhole shaping. Bind off 2 sts at armhole edge. Dec 1 st at armhole edge of next row and every foll row 0 (0, 1, 1, 2) times.

SHOULDER SHAPING

Bind off 2 sts at armhole edge twice. Bind of rem sts.

Rejoin yarn and work second side to match, reversing shaping.

FINISHING

Seam right shoulder. Using size US 17 (12mm) circular needle, pick up and k13 (14, 14, 15, 15) sts down left front, 13 (14, 14, 15, 15) sts up right front, and 16 (18, 18, 20, 20) sts across back (42 [46, 46, 50, 50] sts). Work in k1, p1 rib for 1 row, then bind off. Join left shoulder and side seams.

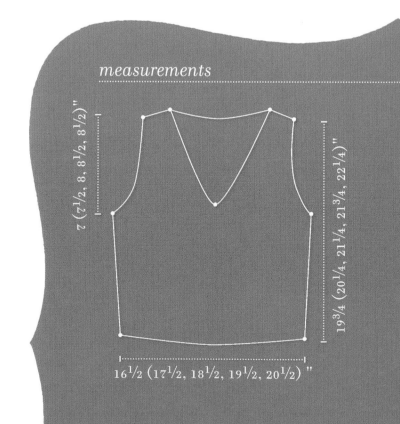

measurements

7 (7½, 8, 8½, 8½)"

19¾ (20¼, 21¼, 21¾, 22¼)"

16½ (17½, 18½, 19½, 20½)"

TIP

When working with super large needles, it can be difficult to get an accurate gauge. Consider making a smaller or larger size if you have trouble getting gauge.

k.i.s.s.

{ KEEP-IT-SIMPLE-SO-YOUR-MAN-WILL-WEAR-IT SWEATER }

When I began this sweater, I had all kinds of ideas for it. I toyed with the concept of a side-to-side construction. I thought about using several colors. On and on and on. Later, I wondered if the average guy would wear the garment I envisioned. I discussed my ideas with some men I know (and with the people who knit for them) and the general consensus was that I should keep it simple, so a man would want to wear it. Hence, the K.I.S.S. sweater was born—a simple, roll-neck pullover knit with a subtle variegated yarn.

CONSTRUCTION NOTES

This simple sweater is constructed in separate pieces that are sewn together at the end. Basic ribbing around the waistband and wrists as well as the natural curl of the stockinette neckline add a little subtle shaping.

MEASUREMENTS

TO FIT CHEST

SMALL	38" (97CM)
MEDIUM	40" (102CM)
LARGE	42" (107CM)
X-LARGE	44" (112CM)
XX-LARGE	46" (117CM)

YARN

11 (13, 14, 15, 17) skeins
South West Trading Company Karaoke
#284 Essence

NEEDLES

size US 7 (4.5mm) needles

size US 6 (4mm) needles

If necessary, change needle size to obtain correct gauge.

NOTIONS

stitch holders

GAUGE

18 sts and 29 rows = 4" (10cm) in stockinette stitch on size 7 (4.5mm) needles

BACK

With size US 6 (4mm) needles, CO 95 (100, 105, 110, 115) sts. Work in k2, p3 rib for 14 rows. Change to size US 7 (4.5mm) needles, and cont in stockinette until piece measures 15¼ (15½, 15½, 16, 16)" (39 [39, 39, 41, 41]cm) from cast-on edge.

ARMHOLE SHAPING

Bind off 4 sts at beg of next 2 rows (87 [92, 97, 102, 107] sts).

Working all dec as follows, k2, k2tog, knit to last 4 sts, k2tog tbl, k2, dec 1 st at each end of next and foll alt rows 3 times (79 [84, 89, 94, 99] sts). Cont straight in stockinette until armhole measures 9½ (9¾, 10, 10½, 11)" (24 [25, 26, 27, 28]cm), ending with a WS row.

SHOULDER AND NECK SHAPING

Bind off 7 (8, 8, 9, 10) sts at beg of next 2 rows.

Bind off 7 (7, 8, 9, 9) sts, and knit until there are 10 (11, 12, 12, 13) sts on right-hand needle. Turn and bind off 4 sts, purl to end of row. Bind off all rem sts. Place center 31 (32, 33, 34, 35) sts on a holder, rejoin yarn and knit to end. Work second side to match first side, reversing shaping.

FRONT

Work as for back until armhole measures 6¾ (7, 7⅓, 7¾, 8½)" (17 [18, 19, 20, 211]cm).

NECK AND SHOULDER SHAPING

Knit 26 (28, 30, 32, 34) sts and turn. Place rem sts on a holder. Dec 1 st at neck edge on next 2 rows and every foll alt row 4 times (20 [22, 24, 26, 28] sts). Work 3 rows in stockinette.

Bind off 7 (8, 8, 9, 10) sts at armhole edge once, then bind off 7 (7, 8, 9, 9) sts at armhole edge once. Work 1 row. Bind off rem sts.

With RS facing, leave center 27 (28, 29, 30, 31) sts on holder, replace rem 26 (28, 30, 32, 34) sts on needle, rejoin yarn and knit to end. Work to match first side, reversing shaping.

SLEEVES

With size US 6 (4mm) needles, CO 50 (50, 55, 55, 60) sts. Work in k2, p3 rib for 14 rows. Change to size US 7 (4.5mm) needles, and cont in stocki-nette, inc 1 st at each end of next row and every foll sixth row 15 (16, 15, 17, 17) times (82 [84, 87, 91, 96] sts).

Cont straight until piece mesasures 20½ (21½, 21½, 22¼, 22¼)" (52 [55, 55, 57, 57]cm) from cast-on edge.

Bind off 4 sts at beg of next 2 rows (74 [76, 79, 83, 88] sts).

Working all dec as follows, k2, k2tog, knit to last 4 sts, k2tog tbl, k2, dec 1 st at each end of next and every foll alt row 4 times (64 [66, 69, 73, 78] sts). Work 1 row. Bind off all rem sts.

FINISHING

Sew right shoulder seam

NECKBAND

With RS facing and using smaller nee-dles, pick up and k10 sts down left front side of neck, 27 (28, 29, 30, 31) sts from front stitch holder, 10 sts up right front side of neck, 4 sts down right back side of neck, 31 (32, 33, 34, 35) sts from back stitch holder, and 4 sts up left back side of neck (86 [88, 90, 92, 94] sts).

Beg with a purl row, work in stockinette for 2" (5cm), ending with a RS row. Bind off loosely. Collar will roll outward natu-rally. Weave in ends.

NOTES: *placing stitches on a holder*

Most sweater patterns worked from the bottom up require that you place some of the front and back neck stitches onto a holder as you bind off the shoulder stitches. You may buy a stitch holder and slide the stitches onto it, or just use a piece of scrap yarn in a contrasting color. The stitches will be picked back up at the end to make a neckband.

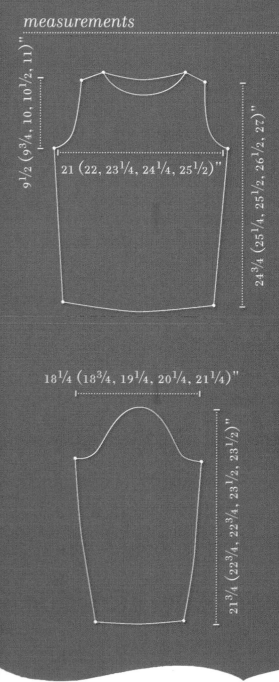

9½ (9¾, 10, 10½, 11)"

21 (22, 23¼, 24¼, 25½)"

24¾ (25¼, 25½, 26½, 27)"

18¼ (18¾, 19¼, 20¼, 21¼)"

21¾ (22¾, 22¾, 23½, 23½)"

chelsea
{ DROP-SHOULDER PULLOVER }

For most of my knitting life, I didn't have much love for the drop shoulder. That is until I saw Sarah Jessica Parker wearing one in an episode of "Sex and The City" a few years ago. I couldn't believe how up-to-the-minute-hip it looked on her. Had I missed the memo? Were stylish women all over the world wearing drop-shoulder pullovers and no one bothered to let me know?

CONSTRUCTION NOTES

Since this sweater has minimal shaping, it's a perfect first sweater. And there's plenty of space over which to perfect your reverse stockinette stitch.

MEASUREMENTS

TO FIT BUST	
X-SMALL	32" (81CM)
SMALL	34" (86CM)
MEDIUM	36" (91CM)
LARGE	38" (97CM)
X-LARGE	40" (102CM)

YARN

10 (10, 11, 12, 12) skeins Artyarns Supermerino
   #135 variegated orange (MC)

2 (2, 2, 3, 3) skeins Artyarns Supermerino
   #116 tangerine (CC)

NEEDLES

size US 9 (5.5mm) needles
16" (40cm) size US 9 (5.5mm) circular needle

If necessary, change needle size to obtain correct gauge.

NOTIONS

stitch holders
safety pins

GAUGE

19 sts and 29 rows = 4" (10cm) in reverse stockinette stitch

BACK

With size US 9 (5.5mm) needles and MC, CO 84 (90, 94, 99, 103) sts. Work in reverse stockinette (purl on RS, knit on WS) until piece measures 13 (14, 14, 14, 14, 14½)" (33 [36, 36, 36, 37]cm) from cast-on edge.

Place a safety pin at each edge of the knitted piece to mark the start of the armholes. Cont straight in reverse stockinette until armholes measure 8¼ (8¾, 9, 9½, 9¾)" (21 [22, 23, 24, 25]cm) from marker.

NECK SHAPING

Bind off 26 (28, 30, 31, 33) sts, place center 32 (34, 34, 37, 37) sts on holder, rejoin yarn and bind off rem 26 (28, 30, 31, 33) sts.

FRONT

Work as for back until armholes measure 5¾ (6¼, 6¾, 7¼, 7½)" (15 [16, 17, 18, 19]cm) from safety pin marker, ending with a WS row.

NECK SHAPING

NEXT ROW: Purl 34 (36, 38, 39, 41) sts, place center 16 (18, 18, 21, 21) sts on holder. Add an additional skein of yarn and work rem 34 (36, 38, 39, 41) sts.

Working each side of neck separately, dec 1 st at neck edge of next and every foll alt row 7 times (26 [28, 30, 31, 33] sts each shoulder).

Work 2 rows in reverse stockinette stitch.

Bind off all sts on both sides of neck.

SLEEVES

With size US 9 (5.5mm) needles and CC, CO 48 (48, 48, 54, 54) sts. Work in k3, p3 rib for 4½" (12cm). Change to MC and cont in reverse stockinette for an additional 4½" (12cm).

Inc 1 st at each end of next and every foll eighth row 12 (8, 4, 4, 0) times, then every seventh row 0 (6, 11, 11, 16) times (74 [78, 80, 86, 88] sts). Cont straight in reverse stockinette stitch until piece measures 25" (64cm) from cast-on edge.

Bind off all sts.

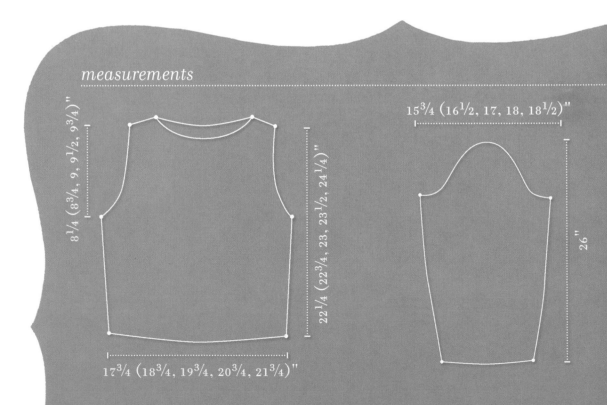

measurements

8¼ (8¾, 9, 9½, 9¾)"

15¾ (16½, 17, 18, 18½)"

22¼ (22¾, 23, 23½, 24¼)"

26"

17¾ (18¾, 19¾, 20¾, 21¾)"

FINISHING

Sew shoulder seams. Sew sleeve caps to armhole edges, matching sleeve edges to safety pin markers. Sew sleeve and side seams.

COLLAR

With 16" (40cm) size US 9 (5.5mm) circular needle and CC, pick up and knit 32 (34, 34, 37, 37) sts from back stitch holder, 16 sts down left front, 16 (18, 18, 21, 21) sts from front stitch holder and 16 sts up right front (80 [84, 84, 90, 90] sts). Join sts for working in the round.

NEXT RND: *k6, knit into front and back of next stitch; repeat from * 10 (12, 12, 12, 12) times, k to end of round (90 [96, 96, 102, 102] sts).

Work in k3, p3 rib until collar measures 8" (20cm). Bind off all sts loosely. Weave in ends.

When I designed this piece I was listening to early Bowie and The Velvet Underground. I was thinking about London's Carnaby Street in the 60s and Andy Warhol's Factory in New York City and how much the art, music and fashion of that era has influenced my taste and aesthetic. Tragic icons like Nico and Edie Sedgwick with their good-girl-gone-bad looks are permanently etched into my consciousness. This cardigan is a marriage of the sometimes severe and often playful looks the 60s underground introduced into the mainstream.

edie
{ ASYMMETRICAL CARDIGAN }

CONSTRUCTION NOTES

Knit with two complementary colors and asymmetrical shaping, Edie adds a twist to the traditional cardigan. The super-easy embroidery kicks it up a notch, giving it a fun "what's-old-is-new-again" vibe. Wear Edie with cuffed jeans and a pair of loafers for a cool, retro look!

MEASUREMENTS

TO FIT BUST

X-SMALL	32" (81CM)
SMALL	34" (86CM)
MEDIUM	36" (91CM)
LARGE	38" (97CM)
X-LARGE	40" (102CM)

YARN

2 (2, 2, 2, 3) skeins Lorna's Laces Fisherman
#22 Turquoise (MC)

1 skein Lorna's Laces Fisherman
#6 Douglas Fir (CC)

NEEDLES

size US 8 (5mm) needles
size US 6 (4mm) needles

If necessary, change needle size to obtain correct gauge.

NOTIONS

seven ¾" (2cm) buttons

GAUGE

20 sts and 30 rows = 4" (10cm) on size 8 (5mm) needles in stockinette stitch

BACK

With size US 6 (4mm) needles and MC, CO 88 (92, 98, 102, 108) sts. Work in k1, p1 rib for 10 rows. Change to size US 8 (5mm) needles and work 4 rows in stockinette.

NEXT ROW: k2, k2tog, knit to last 4 sts, k2tog tbl, k2. Rep this row every foll sixth row 3 times (80 [84, 90, 94, 100] sts).

Work 15 rows straight in stockinette, ending with a WS row.

NEXT ROW: k2, m1, knit to last 2 sts, m1, k2. Rep this row every foll tenth row 3 times (88 [92, 98, 102, 108] sts).

Cont straight in stockinette until back measures 13 (13, 13½, 13½, 14)" (33 [33, 34, 34, 36]cm) from cast-on edge, ending with a WS row.

ARMHOLE SHAPING

Bind off 5 (5, 5, 6, 6) sts at beg of next 2 rows.

NEXT ROW: k2, k2tog, knit to last 4 sts, k2tog tbl, k2.

NEXT ROW: p2, p2tog tbl, purl to last 4 sts, p2tog tbl, p2.

Working all dec as set, dec 1 st at each end of next row, then every foll alt row 2 (3, 5, 4, 6) times (68 [70, 72, 76, 78] sts).

Cont straight in stockinette until arm-holes measure 7¼ (7¾, 8¼, 8½, 9)" (18½ [20, 21, 21½, 23]cm).

SHOULDER AND NECK SHAPING

Bind off 6 (6, 6, 7, 7) sts at beg of next 2 rows.

Bind off 6 (6, 6, 7, 7) sts at beg of next row, knit until there are 11 sts on right hand needle. Turn and bind off 4 sts, purl to end. Bind off rem sts.

Rejoin yarn, cast off center 22 (24, 26, 26, 28) sts, knit to end. Complete to match first side, reversing shaping.

LEFT FRONT

With size US 6 (4mm) needles and CC, CO 38 (40, 44, 46, 48) sts. Work in k1, p1 rib for 10 rows. Change to size US 8 (5mm) needles and work 4 rows in stockinette, dec 0 (0, 1, 1, 0) st on first row (38 [40, 43, 45, 48] sts).

NEXT ROW: k2, k2tog, knit to end of row. Rep this row every foll sixth row 3 times (34 [36, 39, 41, 44] sts).

Work 15 rows straight in stockinette, ending with a WS row.

NEXT ROW: K2, m1, knit to end of row. Rep this row every foll tenth row 3 times (38 [40, 43, 45, 48] sts).

Cont straight until left front measures 13 (13, 13½, 13½, 14)" (33 [33, 34, 34, 36]cm) from cast-on edge, ending with a WS row.

ARMHOLE SHAPING

Bind off 5 (5, 5, 6, 6) sts at beg of row, knit to end of row. Purl 1 row.

NEXT ROW: k2, k2tog, knit to end of row.

NEXT ROW: purl to last 4 sts, p2tog, p2.

Working all dec as set, dec 1 st at arm-hole edge of next row, then every alt row 2 (3, 5, 4, 6) times (28 [29, 30, 32, 33] sts).

Cont straight in stockinette until arm-hole measure 5½ (6, 6½, 6¾, 7¼)" (14 [15, 16, 17, 18]cm).

NECK SHAPING

Bind off 3 sts at neck edge once, then bind off 2 sts once. Dec 1 st at neck edge every alt row 3 times, then every row 1 (2, 3, 3, 4) times (19 [19, 19, 21, 21] sts).

At the same time, when armhole mea-sures 7¼ (7¾, 8¼, 8½, 9)" (19 [21, 22, 23]cm), begin shoulder shaping.

SHOULDER SHAPING

Bind off 6 (6, 6, 7, 7) sts at armhole edge twice. Work 1 row. Bind off rem sts.

NOTES: *k2tog tbl or p2tog tbl*

To knit two together through the back loop, insert the right needle into the back loops of the first two stitches on the left-hand needle. Wrap the yarn and knit as usual. To purl two together through the back loop, slip the right needle into the back loops of the first two stitches on the left needle from back to front. Wrap the yarn and purl as usual.

RIGHT FRONT

With size US 6 (4mm) needles and MC, CO 50 (52, 56, 58, 60) sts. Work in k1, p1 rib for 10 rows. Change to size US 8 (5mm) needles and work 4 rows in stockinette, dec 0 (0,1, 1, 0) st on first row (50 [52, 55, 57, 60] sts).

NEXT ROW: knit to last 4 sts, k2tog tbl, k2. Rep this row every foll sixth row 3 times (46 [48, 51, 53, 56] sts).

Work 15 rows straight in stockinette, ending with a WS row.

NEXT ROW: knit to last 2 sts, m1, k2. Rep this row every foll tenth row 3 times (50 [52, 55, 57, 60] sts).

Cont straight until piece measures 13 (13, 13½, 13½, 14)" (33 [33, 34, 34, 36]cm) from cast-on edge, ending with a RS row.

ARMHOLE SHAPING

Bind off 5 (5, 5, 6, 6) sts at beg of next row. Knit 1 row.

NEXT ROW: p2, p2tog tbl, purl to end of row.

NEXT ROW: knit to last 4 sts, k2tog tbl, k2.

Working all dec as set, dec 1 st at armhole edge of next row, then every alt row 2 (3, 5, 4, 6) times (40 [41, 42, 44, 45] sts).

Cont straight in stockinette until armhole measures 5½ (6, 6½, 6¾, 7¼)" (14 [15, 16, 17, 18]cm).

NECK SHAPING

Bind off 15 sts at neck edge once, then bind off 2 sts at neck edge once. Dec 1 st at neck edge every alt row 3 times, then every row 1 (2, 3, 3, 4) time(s) (19 [19, 21, 21] sts).

At the same time, when armhole measures 7¼ (7¾, 8¼, 8½, 9)" (19 [20, 21, 22, 23]cm), begin shoulder shaping.

SHOULDER SHAPING

Bind off 6 (6, 6, 7, 7) sts at armhole edge twice. Work 1 row. Bind off rem sts.

SLEEVES

With size US 6 (4mm) needles and CC, CO 38 (40, 40, 42, 44) sts. Work in k1, p1 rib for 16 rows. Switch to size US 8 (5mm) needles and MC, and work in stockinette, inc 1 st at each end of next and every foll eighth row 10 (10, 12, 13, 13) times (60 [62, 66, 70, 72] sts). Cont straight until piece measures 18 (18½, 19, 19, 19½)" (46 [47, 48, 48, 50]cm) from cast-on edge.

SHAPE SLEEVE CAPS

Bind off 5 (5, 5, 6, 6) sts at beg of next 2 rows (50 [52, 56, 58, 60] sts).

NEXT ROW: k2, k2tog, knit to last 4 sts, k2tog tbl, k2.

NEXT ROW: p2, p2tog tbl, purl to last 4 sts, p2tog, p2.

Working all dec as set, dec 1 st at each end of next and every foll alt row 14 (15, 17, 18, 19) times (16 sts). Bind off all rem sts.

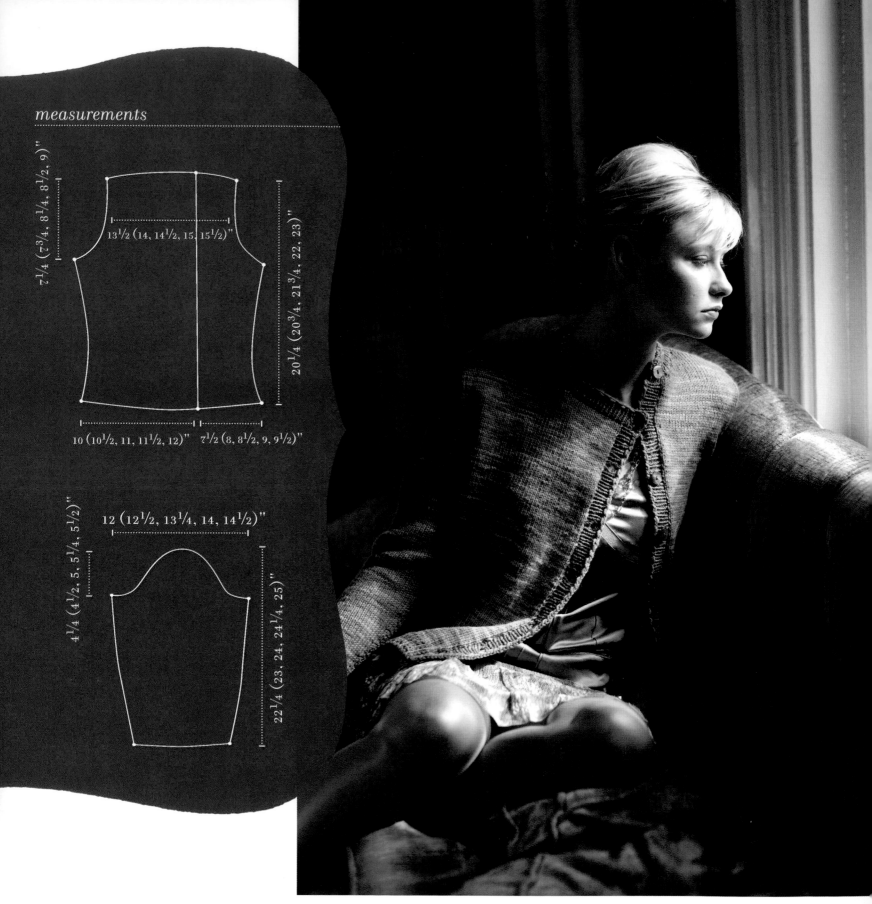

measurements

$7^1/4$ $(7^3/4, 8^1/4, 8^1/2, 9)$"

$13^1/2$ $(14, 14^1/2, 15, 15^1/2)$"

$20^1/4$ $(20^3/4, 21^3/4, 22, 23)$"

10 $(10^1/2, 11, 11^1/2, 12)$" $7^1/2$ $(8, 8^1/2, 9, 9^1/2)$"

12 $(12^1/2, 13^1/4, 14, 14^1/2)$"

$4^1/4$ $(4^1/2, 5, 5^1/4, 5^1/2)$"

$22^1/4$ $(23, 24, 24^1/4, 25)$"

FINISHING

BUTTON BAND

With size US 6 (4mm) needles and CC, with RS facing, pick up and k96 (98, 102, 104, 108) sts along left front edge. Work in k1, p1 rib for 3 rows. Bind off.

BUTTONHOLE BAND

With size US 6 (4mm) needles and CC, with RS facing, pick up and k96 (98, 102, 104, 108) sts along right front edge. Work in k1, p1 rib for 3 rows.

BUTTONHOLE ROW: rib 4 (5, 4, 5, 4), yo, work 2 tog, *rib 14 (14, 15, 15, 16) sts, yo, work 2 tog; rep from * 4 times, rib to end. Work in k1, p1 rib for 3 rows. Bind off all sts.

Seam shoulders.

NECKBAND

With size US 6 (4mm) needles and CC, with RS facing, pick up and knit 5 sts across top of right front button band, 15 across right front, 15 up right front neck, 30 (32, 34, 36) across back neck, 15 down left front neck, 3 across left front, and 5 across top of left front buttonhole band (88 [90, 92, 94] sts).

Work in k1, p1 rib for 3 rows.

NEXT ROW: rib 3, yo, work 2 tog. Cont in rib until end of row.

Work 3 more rows in rib and then bind off.

FINAL PIECING

Set in sleeves. Sew side and sleeve seams. Using CC, loosely work a running stitch around edges of garment, working over two rows and under one (see Notes, this page).

NOTES: *running stitch*

Using a darning needle and CC, bring needle up from wrong side to right side of fabric. Bring yarn across a couple of stitches, working from right to left. Bring needle back through to wrong side of fabric. Skip one or two knit stitches between running stitches.

I was raised to believe that white should never be worn after Labor Day. Similarly, I am sure a few knitters may cry 'Heresy!' to find that this spring/summer-weight garment includes a little wool. This is 'The New Knitting'! Just as I learned to embrace winter whites, you, too, can expand your ideas about what to wear and when to wear it. It's important to explore our own ways to design and to knit. Blindly following patterns and knitting what everyone else is knitting has never been an option for me. If this is a knitting revolution, we should knit as we see fit!

lorelei
{ TANK TOP }

CONSTRUCTION NOTES

The bottom part of Lorelei is knit in a strip from side to side in stockinette with occasional eyelet rows and garter stitch ridges. Make this design your own by adding these variations wherever you like.

MEASUREMENTS

TO FIT BUST	
X-SMALL	32" (81CM)
SMALL	34" (86CM)
MEDIUM	36" (91CM)
LARGE	38" (97CM)
X-LARGE	40" (102CM)

YARN
5 (5, 5, 6, 6) skeins Noro Lily
   #18 muted violet

1 skein Noro Silk Garden
   #224 variegated purples and greens

NEEDLES
29" (74cm) size US 8 (5mm) circular needle

If necessary, change needle size to obtain correct gauge.

NOTIONS
stitch holders

size H (5mm) crochet hook

GAUGE
20 sts and 30 rows = 4" (10cm) in stockinette stitch with MC

BOTTOM PANEL

With MC and size US 8 (5mm) needle, cast on 56 (58, 58, 60, 60) sts. Work in stockinette stitch with occasional garter and eyelet rows until piece measures 31½ (33½, 35½, 37½, 29½)" (80 [85, 90, 96, 100]cm) from cast-on ege. Bind off all sts.

Sew cast-on edge to bind-off edge, forming a tube. Lay piece flat with seam on left side. Find halfway point (right side fold) and place marker.

TOP OF TANK

With MC and size US 8 (5mm) circular needle, beg at side seam, pick up and k156 (164, 176, 184, 196) sts around top of tube. Join yarn for working in the round.

NEXT ROUND: * p8, p2tog; rep from * 14 (15, 16, 17, 18) times. p6 (4, 6, 4, 6) (141 [148, 159, 166, 177] sts).

CHANGE TO CC and knit 1 rnd. Work in seed stitch for 5 (5, 5, 7, 7) rnds. Knit 1 rnd.

NEXT ROUND: Change to MC and *k9, m1; rep from * to 14 (15, 16, 17, 18) times, k6 (4, 6, 4, 6) (156 [164, 176, 184, 196] sts). Cont in stockinette stitch until piece measures 13½ (14, 14, 14½, 14½)" (34 [36, 36, 37, 37]cm) from lower edge.

Divide sts evenly for front and back, placing 78 (82, 88, 92, 98) sts on holder and keeping 78 (82, 88, 92, 98) sts for back on needle.

NOTES: *details*

KNITTED EFFECTS

EYELET ROW: k4, * yo, sl1, k1, psso, k2; rep from * to last 4 (6, 6, 4, 4) sts, knit to end.

GARTER RIDGE: knit 1 row on wrong side or purl 1 row on right side.

GARTER AND EYELET MOTIF

To create a garter and eyelet motif, knit the rows described above in the following sequence: garter ridge, 3 rows stockinette, eyelet row, 3 rows stockinette, garter ridge. Intersperse this motif wherever you like in your Lorelei.

SLIP STITCH CROCHET

On right side of fabric, with edge facing away from you, insert hook into top edge of stitch, wrap yarn over hook and pull through fabric. * Insert hook into next stitch, wrap yarn over hook, pull through the fabric and through the loop on hook. Rep from * to create a border as desired.

SINGLE CROCHET

On right side of fabric, with edge facing away from you, insert hook into top edge of stitch, wrap yarn over hook and pull through fabric, wrap yarn over hook and pull through loop. * Insert hook into next stitch, wrap yarn over hook and pull through both loops on hook. Rep from * as desired.

BACK

ARMHOLE SHAPING
Bind off 5 (5, 5, 6, 6) sts at beg of next 2 rows. Dec 1 st each end of next and every foll alt row 1 (2, 3, 4, 6) time(s) (64 [68, 70, 70, 72] sts). Cont straight in stockinette until armholes measure 2½ (2½, 3, 3, 3)" (6 [6, 8, 8, 8]cm).

NECK SHAPING
NEXT ROW (RS): k30 (32, 33, 33, 34), k2tog, turn, place rem 32 (34, 35, 35, 36) sts on a holder. Dec 1 st at neck edge every foll alt row 8 times, then every row 12 (14, 14, 14, 14) times (11 [11, 12, 12, 13] sts). Cont straight in stockinette until armholes measure 7 (7¼, 7½, 7¾, 8)" (18 [19, 19, 20, 21]cm).

SHOULDER SHAPING
Bind off 6 (6, 7, 7, 7) sts at armhole edge, work to end. Bind off rem sts.

Rejoin yarn and work second side to match.

FRONT
Transfer stitches from holder to needle and rejoin yarn.

ARMHOLE SHAPING
Bind off and dec as for back. Cont straight in stockinette until armholes measure 1¾ (1¾, 1¾, 2½, 2¼)" (5 [5, 5, 6, 6]cm).

NECK SHAPING
NEXT ROW (RS): k30 (32, 33, 33, 34), k2tog, turn, place rem 32 (34, 35, 35, 36) sts on a holder. Dec 1 st at neck edge every foll alt row 16 times, then ever row 4 (6, 6, 6, 6) times (11 [11, 12, 12, 13] sts). Cont straight in stockinette until armholes measure 7 (7¼, 7½, 7¾, 8)" (18 [19, 19, 20, 21]cm).

FINISHING
Sew shoulder seams.

CROCHET BORDER
With MC and size H crochet hook, work 1 row of slip stitch around neckline, then 1 row of single crochet (see Notes, page 96).

With CC and size H crochet hook, work 1 row of slip stitch around armholes, skipping every fifth stitch.

With CC and size H crochet hook, work 1 row of slip stitch around hem, skipping every fifth stitch, then work 1 row of single crochet.

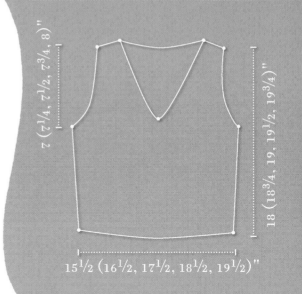

measurements

7 (7¼, 7½, 7¾, 8)"

18 (18¾, 19, 19½, 19¾)"

15½ (16½, 17½, 18½, 19½)"

Last spring I found myself staring at a beautiful pile of yarn scraps and leftover skeins that were too precious to discard, but there wasn't enough of any single one to knit an entire garment. I decided to incorporate them all into one knitted piece, using the same basic construction as for Lorelei. I chose two yarns whose palettes overlap, thus providing a vast range of interesting color combinations to choose from. As I worked on the bottom strip, I experimented with adding garter ridges and striped portions. I knit the bottom section predominantly with one yarn and the top with another.

poppy
{ V-NECK PULLOVER }

CONSTRUCTION NOTES

The bottom part of Poppy is knit in a strip from side to side. It is knit in stockinette with occasional stockinette stripes, as well as occasional rows of garter stitch. Make this design your own by using these variations wherever you like. If you decide to knit more than a quarter of this section with Silk Garden you may need to purchase additional yarn.

MEASUREMENTS

TO FIT BUST

X-SMALL	32" (81CM)
SMALL	34" (86CM)
MEDIUM	36" (91CM)
LARGE	38" (97CM)
X-LARGE	40" (102CM)

YARN

6 (6, 7, 7, 8) skeins Silk Garden,
   #84 variegated reds and browns (MC)

3 (3, 4, 4, 4) skeins Cash Iroha
   #91 red (CC)

NEEDLES

29" (74cm) size US 8 (5mm)
circular needle

size US 8 (5mm) dpn

If necessary, change needle size to obtain correct gauge.

NOTIONS

stitch holders

size H (5mm) crochet hook

removable marker or safety pin

GAUGE

18 sts and 29 rows = 4" (10cm) in stockinette stitch with MC

18 sts and 28 rows = 4" (10cm) in stockinette stitch with CC

BOTTOM PANEL

With 29" (74cm) US 8 (5mm) circular needle and CC, CO 56 (58, 60, 62) sts. Work in stockinette stitch, adding garter stitch ridges (as desired) and occasional stockinette stripes in MC. Cont to work straight until piece measures 33½ (35½, 37½, 39½, 41½)" (85 [90, 95, 100, 105]cm). Bind off all sts.

Sew cast-on edge to bind-off edge, forming a tube. Lay piece flat with seam at center back. Mark right side fold.

TOP OF PULLOVER

Using 29" (74cm) US size 8 (5mm) circular needle and MC, beg at right side marker, pick up and k148 (156, 168, 176, 184) sts evenly spaced around top of bottom panel. Purl 1 rnd. Knit 1 rnd.

Divide sts evenly for front and back, placing 74 (78, 84, 88, 92) sts for front on holder and leaving 74 (78, 84, 88, 92) sts for back on needle.

BACK

ARMHOLE SHAPING

Bind off 4 (4, 5, 5, 6) sts at beg of next 2 rows. Dec 1 st at armhole edge of next row, then every other row 2 (3, 4, 5, 5) times (60 [62, 64, 66, 68] sts). Cont straight in stockinette stitch until armholes measure 7¾ (8¼, 8½, 8¾, 9)" (20 [21, 22, 22, 23]cm).

SHOULDER SHAPING

Bind off 6 sts at beg of next 4 rows. Bind off 5 (6, 6, 7, 7) sts at beg of next 2 rows. Bind off rem 26 (26, 28, 28, 30) sts for back of neck.

FRONT

Transfer stitches from holder to needle and rejoin yarn.

ARMHOLE SHAPING

Bind off and decrease as for back (60 [62, 64, 66, 68] sts).

NECK SHAPING

NEXT ROW (RS): k28 (29, 30, 31, 32) sts, k2tog, turn, leaving rem sts on a holder. Dec 1 st at neck edge on next and every foll third row 11 (11, 12, 12, 12) times (17 [18, 18, 19, 19] sts). Cont straight in stockinette, if necessary, until armholes measure 7¾ (8¼, 8½, 8¾, 9)" (20 [21, 22, 22, 23]cm).

SHOULDER SHAPING

Bind off 6 sts at armhole edge twice. Work 1 row. Bind off rem 5 (6, 6, 7, 7) sts.

Rejoin yarn, k2tog, knit to end of row. Complete second side to match, reversing shaping.

SLEEVES

note: For a shorter sleeve, work 1–2 fewer rounds between increases.

With size US 8 (5mm) dpn and CC, CO 50 (52, 55, 57, 59) sts. Join yarn for working in the round, taking care not to twist sts.

RND 1: Knit.

RND 2: Purl.

RNDS 3–4: Rep Rnds 1–2.

RND 5: Knit.

Change to MC and knit 3 rows. Cont in stockinette, dec 1 st at beg and end of next and every foll eighth rnd 4 times (40 [42, 45, 47, 49] sts). Work 10 rnds straight. Inc 1 st at beg and end of next and every foll ninth rnd 7 times (56 [58, 61, 63, 65] sts). Work straight until piece measures 20 (20, 20 20½, 20½)" (51 [51, 51, 52, 52]cm) from cast-on edge.

SHAPE SLEEVE CAPS

Bind off 4 (4, 5, 5, 6) sts at beg of next 2 rows (50 [50, 55] sts). Dec 1 st at each end of next and every foll alt row 13 (13, 13, 14, 14) times, then every row 4 times (12 [14, 15, 15, 15] sts). Work 1 row even. Bind off rem sts.

FINISHING

Join shoulder seams. Set in sleeves. Sew side seams. Weave in ends.

With MC and size H crochet hook, work 1 round of single crochet around front neckline.

With MC and size H crochet hook, work 1 round of slip stitch and then 1 round of single crochet around hem (see Glossary, page 120).

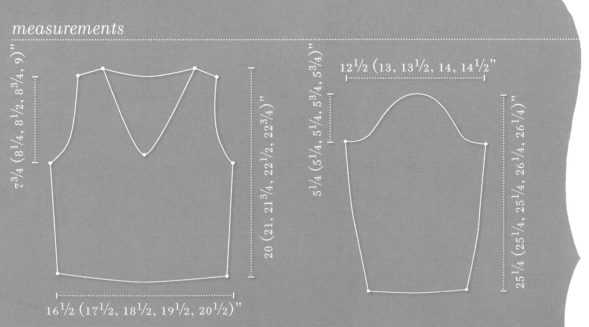

measurements

7³/4 (8¹/4, 8¹/2, 8³/4, 9)"

20 (21, 21³/4, 22¹/2, 22³/4)"

16¹/2 (17¹/2, 18¹/2, 19¹/2, 20¹/2)"

12¹/2 (13, 13¹/2, 14, 14¹/2"

5¹/4 (5¹/4, 5¹/4, 5³/4, 5³/4)"

25¹/4 (25¹/4, 25¹/4, 26¹/4, 26¹/4)"

everything
but the kitchen sink
{ STRIPED SWEATER }

I am a jeans and boots kind of girl, so I expect my sweaters to make a bold statement. And nothing makes a statement like color! I knit the Everything But The Kitchen Sink pullover with about 37 different colors and textures of predominantly aran weight yarns. The more colors and textures, the better! For this design, I suggest a minimum of 18 different shades. You can stick to one color family or you can use every color that appeals to you.

CONSTRUCTION NOTES

The yardage of each yarn can vary from enough for one round to a full skein. In order to keep gauge, the majority of yarns should be the same weight. You can knit an occasional round with a yarn that is slightly lighter or heavier. Occasional deviation from gauge produces an interesting texture. However, you should not use these yarns for more than two rounds at a time.

MEASUREMENTS

TO FIT BUST	
X-SMALL	32" (81CM)
SMALL	34" (86CM)
MEDIUM	36" (91CM)
LARGE	38" (97CM)
X-LARGE	40" (102CM)

YARN

approx 1175 (1250, 1320, 1425, 1510) yards of aran weight yarn

SOME YARNS USED IN THIS SWEATER:

South West Trading Company Karaoke
  #289 Bluezzz

Noro Kureyon
  #166 variegated blue, purple, green

Debbie Bliss Merino Aran
  #208 periwinkle
  #702 navy

Berroco Air
  #3140 variegated blues

Berroco Medley
  #8913 variegated purples

Alchemy Yarns Lone Star
  Deep Sea

NEEDLES

29" (74cm) size US 8 (5mm) circular needle

size US 8 (5mm) dpn

24" (60cm) size US 7 (4.5mm) circular needle

If necessary, change needle size to obtain correct gauge.

NOTIONS

stitch holders

GAUGE

18 sts and 28 rows = 4" (10cm) in stockinette on size US 8 (5mm) needles

note: This garment is knit in the round from the bottom up to the armholes, where the work is divided for front and back. The sleeves are knit in the round as well. Constructing a sweater in this way makes it virtually seamless—practically zero sewing things together at the end. Just a little bit of stitching under the arms, and you're done.

BODY

CO 144 (152, 160, 172, 180) sts with size US 8 (5mm) circular needle. Join sts for working in the rnd, taking care not to twist sts. Work in k2, p2 rib for 7" (18cm). Cont in stockinette until entire piece measures 12 (12½, 12½, 13, 13)" (30 [32, 32, 33, 33]cm) from cast-on edge.

SEPARATE FRONT AND BACK

Place 72 (76, 80, 86, 90) sts for front of garment on stitch holder. Leave rem 72 (76, 80, 86, 90) sts on needle.

BACK

RAGLAN SHAPING

Bind off 5 sts at beg of next 2 rows.

DECREASE AS FOLLOWS: On knit rows, k1, ssk, knit to last 3 sts, k2tog, k1. On purl rows, p1, p2tog tbl, purl to last 3 sts, p2tog, p1.

Dec 1 st at each end of every third row 3 (3, 5, 5, 5) times, then every other row 3 (15, 18, 20) times, then every alt row 14 (16, 15, 18, 20) times. Place rem 26 (26, 27, 27, 29) sts on a holder.

FRONT

Transfer sts from holder onto needle.

RAGLAN SHAPING

Bind off and decrease as for back until 40 (40, 42, 42, 44) sts rem.

NECK SHAPING

NEXT RS ROW: Work in established pattern until there are 13 (13, 14, 14, 14) sts on right-hand needle. Turn. Place rem 26 (26, 27, 27, 29) sts on holder.

Cont raglan decreases at armhole side as established. At the same time, dec 1 st at neck edge of next row, then every other row 4 (4, 5, 5, 5) times. Place rem 2 sts on holder.

Leave center 12 (12, 12, 14, 14) sts on holder and place rem 14 (14, 15, 15, 15) sts onto needle. Rejoin yarn, knit to end. Complete to match first side.

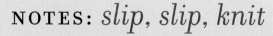

NOTES: *slip, slip, knit*

SLIP, SLIP, KNIT

To create a left-slanting decrease, slip the first stitch as if to knit, slip the second stitch as if to knit, and then bring the right needle through both stitches from front to back and knit the two stitches together.

See the Glossary on pages 120–121 to read about other ways of creating a decrease in the knitted fabric.

JOINING IN NEW YARN

When joining a new yarn, overlap it with the previous yarn and knit with both for three or four stitches. Then cut the first yarn, leaving a 2" (5cm) tail, and continue knitting with the new yarn.

measurements

5½ (6, 6½, 7½, 8)"

17½ (18½, 19, 20½, 21)"

16 (17, 18, 19, 20)"

11 (12, 12½, 13, 13¾)"

24 (24½, 25½, 26½, 27½)"

SLEEVES

Cast on 40 (44, 44, 44, 48) sts on size US 8 (5mm) dpn. Work in k2, p2 rib for 4" (10cm). Inc 1 st at beg and end of next and every foll fourteenth rnd 4 (4, 5, 6, 6) times, working inc into pattern (50 [54, 56, 58, 62] sts). At the same time, when sleeve measures 7½" (19cm), change to stockinette stitch.

When increases are complete, work straight until sleeve measures 18½ (19, 19, 19½, 19½)" (47 [48, 48, 50, 50]cm) from cast-on edge.

RAGLAN SHAPING

Bind off 5 sts at beg of next 2 rows. Dec 1 st at each end as indicated for back every third row 3 (3, 5, 9, 9) times, then every alt row 14 (16, 15, 12, 14) times. Place rem 6 sts on holder.

FINISHING

Sew raglan seams.

COLLAR

With size US 7 (4.5mm) circular needle, k26 (26, 28, 28, 30) sts from back neck holder, knit 6 sts from left sleeve holder, knit 2 sts from front holder, pick up and k11 (11, 12, 11, 12) sts down left front of neck, k12 (12, 12, 14, 14) sts from center front holder, knit 2 sts from front holder, pick up and k11 (11, 12, 11, 12) sts up right front of neck, k2 sts from front holder, knit 6 sts from right sleeve holder (76 [76, 80, 80, 84] sts). Join for working in the round. Work in k2, p2 rib for 8 rnds. Loosely bind off all sts in pattern. Weave in ends.

As a woman whose sole experience with babies is limited to the four-legged kind, I have fairly over-the-top ideas about how little ones should be clothed. Parents are sure to provide plenty of clothing that can survive everyday wear and tear. My job is to provide a stand-out addition to their collection of bibs and onesies. I think of myself as the eccentric godmother who gifts a child with an elegant outfit destined to be a family heirloom. This special garment requires a little extra care, but isn't the baby in your life worth it?

baby a

{ BABY'S HAT + CARDIGAN }

CONSTRUCTION NOTES

The beauty of garter stitch is highly underrated! This purl-free cardigan is worked in side-to-side strips, then stitches are picked up across the top edge and the garment is completed in the usual fashion.

MEASUREMENTS

SWEATER TO FIT AGE

6–9 MOS	22½" (58CM)
9–12 MOS	23½" (60CM)
12–18 MOS	24½" (62CM)

HAT TO FIT AGE

6–9 MOS	14" (36CM)
9–12 MOS	16" (41CM)
12–18 MOS	18" (46CM)

YARN

2 (3, 3) skeins Rowan Felted Tweed
  #154 Ginger (MC)

1 skein Rowan Felted Tweed
  #133 Midnight (MC)

NEEDLES

size US 6 (4mm) needles

size US 4 (3.5mm) needles

size US 5 (3.75mm) dpn

size US 6 (4mm) dpn

If necessary, change needle size to obtain correct gauge.

NOTIONS

six ½" (1cm) buttons

size F (4mm) crochet hook

GAUGE

22 sts and 44 rows = 4" (10cm) on size 6 (4mm) needles in garter stitch

HAT

With CC and size US 5 (3.75mm) dpn, cast on 78 (88, 100) sts. Divide sts evenly over 4 needles and join, taking care not to twist sts. Pm to mark beg of rnd, or use the cast-on tail as marker. Work in k1, p1 rib for 5 rounds.

Switch to MC and size US 6 (4mm) dpn and knit 1 rnd, purl 1 rnd. Cont in garter stitch as established (alternating between knit 1 rnd and purl 1 rnd) until hat measures 4 (5, 6)" (10 [13, 15]cm), ending with a knit row.

NOTES: *placing a marker*

Sometimes a pattern calls for you to place a marker (pm). Markers are generally small plastic rings that slide onto a needle and rest in between stitches, marking a certain spot. When working in the round, you can use a marker to indicate the beginning of each round. If you don't have markers on hand, cut small pieces of scrap yarn in a contrasting color. Tie the scrap yarn in the indicated spot in a loose knot.

See the Glossary on page 121 to read about other ways that stitch markers are used.

CROWN SHAPING

RND 1: * k9, k2 tog; rep from * to end of rnd (70 [80, 90] sts).

RND 2: Purl.

RND 3: * k8, k2 tog; rep from * to end of rnd (63 [72, 81] sts).

RND 4: Purl.

RND 5: * k7, k2 tog; rep from * to end of rnd (56 [64, 72] sts).

RND 6: Purl.

RND 7: * k6, k2 tog; rep from * to end of rnd (49 [56, 63] sts).

RND 8: Purl.

RND 9: * k5, k2 tog; rep from * to end of rnd (42 [48, 54] sts).

RND 10: Purl.

RND 11: * k4, k2 tog; rep from * to end of rnd (35 [40, 45] sts).

RND 12: Purl.

RND 13: * k3, k2 tog; rep from * to end of rnd (28 [32, 36] sts).

RND 14: Purl.

RND 15: * k2, k2 tog; rep from * to end of rnd (21 [24, 27] sts).

RND 16: Purl.

RND 17: * k1, k2 tog (14[16, 18] sts).

RND 18: * p2tog; rep from * to end of rnd (7 [8,9] sts).

Switch to CC, and work 6 (8, 10) rows in garter stitch.

Cut yarn, pull through rem sts, then through top of hat and secure.

CARDIGAN BACK

With CC and size US 6 (4mm) needles, CO 34 (36, 38) sts. Work in garter stitch for 11 (11½, 12)" (28 [29, 31]cm). Bind off all sts.

Turn fabric so the garter ridges are vertical. With MC and size US 6 (4mm) needles, pick up and k60 (64, 68) sts across top of fabric. Work in garter stitch until piece measures 10¼ (11, 12)" (26 [28, 31]cm) from bottom edge.

Bind off 15 (17, 19) sts at beg of next 2 rows. Bind off rem sts.

LEFT FRONT

With CC and size 6 needles, CO 34 (36, 38) sts. Work in garter stitch for 5½ (5¾, 6)" (14 [15, 16]cm). Bind off all sts.

Turn fabric so the garter ridges are vertical. With MC and size 6 needles, pick up and knit 30 (32, 34) sts across top of fabric. Work in garter stitch until piece measures 9½ (10¼, 11¼)" (24 [26, 29]cm) from bottom edge, ending with a right side row.

NECK SHAPING

At beg of next row, bind off 7 sts. Dec 1 st at neck edge every row 8 times. Bind off rem sts.

RIGHT FRONT

Work as for left front, reversing neck shaping.

SLEEVES

With MC and size US 6 (4mm) needles, CO 35 (38, 42) sts. Work in garter stitch for 1¼" (3cm). Inc 1 st at each end of next and every foll seventh row 7 times (51 [54, 58] sts). Work straight until sleeve measures 6½ (7, 7½)" (17 [18, 19]cm). Bind off all sts.

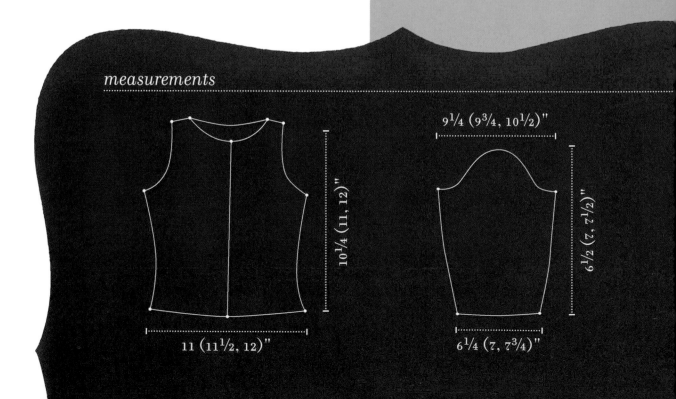

measurements

9¼ (9¾, 10½)"

10¼ (11, 12)"

6½ (7, 7½)"

11 (11½, 12)"

6¼ (7, 7¾)"

112

FINISHING

BUTTON BAND

With size US 4 (3.5mm) needle and MC, with RS facing, pick up and k54 (59, 64) sts along left front edge.

Work in garter stitch for 6 rows. Bind off all sts.

BUTTONHOLE BAND

With size US 4 (3.5mm) needle and MC, with RS facing, pick up and k54 (59, 64) sts along right front edge. Work in garter stitch for 2 rows.

BUTTONHOLE ROW: k3, * yo, k2tog, k7 (8, 9); rep from * 5 times. yo, k2tog, k4.

Work 3 rows in garter stitch. Bind off all sts.

PIECE TOGETHER

Sew sleeves to armhole edges. Sew sleeve and side seams, placing "armpit" at start of MC in body piece. Sew on buttons opposite buttonholes. Weave in ends.

With size F crochet hook and MC, work 1 row of single crochet around neck edge and sleeve cuffs (see Glossary, page 120 for specific instructions on single crochet).

When a student of mine was asked why she didn't knit a sweater her granddaughter could grow into, she replied, "I don't want it to look terrible by the time it actually fits her." This struck me as the smartest thing I'd heard about knitting for kids. The general consensus among knitters is that kids should get as much wear as possible out of a garment. However, they don't seem to consider that it could be outworn by the time it fits. Or that it may look like a paper sack. Fitting in is hard enough for kids, don't make them suffer by forcing them to wear bad knitting!

stripey
{ KID'S SWEATER + HAT }

CONSTRUCTION NOTES

This sweater is made in separate pieces that are sewn together into a sweater. Like Lorelei and Poppy (pages 94 and 98), this sweater begins with a bottom panel from which stitches are picked up. However, instead of working in the round, you'll knit two separate panels and pick up stitches to work each piece flat.

MEASUREMENTS

SWEATER TO FIT AGE

2–3 YRS	28" (55CM)
4–6 YRS	30" (76CM)
7–9 YRS	32" (81CM)
10 YRS	34" (86CM)

HAT TO FIT SIZE

SMALL	17" (36CM)
MEDIUM	19" (41CM)
LARGE	21½" (55CM)

YARN

8 (9, 10, 11) skeins Artyarns Supermerino
  #104 variegated blues and greens (MC)

1 skein Artyarns Supermerino
  #120 dark teal (CC)

NEEDLES

size US 9 (5.5mm) needles

size US 7 (4.5mm) needles

16" (40cm) size US 7 (4.5mm) circular needle

16" (40cm) size US 9 (5.5mm) circular needle

size US 9 (5.5mm) dpn

If necessary, change needle size to obtain correct gauge.

NOTIONS

stitch holders

size H (5mm) crochet hook

GAUGE

20 sts and 27 rows = 4" (10cm) on size 9 (5.5mm) needles in stockinette stitch

HAT

With 16" (41cm) size US 9 (5.5mm) circular needle and CC, cast on 84 (96, 108) sts. Work in k2, p2 rib for 7 rows. Change to MC and cont straight in stockinette for 5½ (6½, 7½)" (14[17, 19]cm).

Change to dpn when sts become stretched too far to comfortably knit.

RND 1: * k10, k2tog; rep from * to end of rnd (77 [88, 99] sts).

RND 2: * k9, k2tog; rep from * to end of rnd (70 [80, 90] sts).

RND 3: * k8, k2tog; rep from * to end of rnd (63 [72, 81] sts).

RND 4: * k7, k2tog; rep from * to end of rnd (56 [64, 72] sts).

RND 5: * k6, k2tog; rep from * to end of rnd (49 [56, 63] sts).

RND 6: * k5, k2tog; rep from * to end of rnd (42 [48, 54] sts).

RND 7: * k4, k2tog; rep from * to end of rnd (35 [40, 45] sts).

RND 8: * k3, k2tog; rep from * to end of rnd (28 [32, 36] sts).

RND 9: * k2, k2tog; rep from * to end of rnd (21 [24, 27] sts).

RND 10: * k1, k2tog; rep from * to end of rnd (14 [16, 18] sts).

RND 11: * k2tog; rep from * to end of rnd (7 [8, 9] sts).

Knit 5 (7, 9) rnds with dpn.

Bind off all sts.

SWEATER

BOTTOM PANEL (MAKE 2)

With MC and 16" (40cm) size US 9 (5.5mm) circular needle, CO 20 (20, 25, 25) sts. Work in stockinette until strip measures 14 (15, 16, 17)" (36 [38, 41, 43]cm). Bind off all sts.

BACK

With 16" (40cm) size US 9 (5.5mm) circular needle and CC, with RS facing, pick up and k70 (75, 80, 85) sts across top of one strip. Work 3 rows in stockinette, beg with a purl row.

Change to MC and cont in stockinette until piece measures 10 (10, 12, 12)" (25 [25, 30, 30]cm) from bottom edge of bottom panel.

ARMHOLE SHAPING

Bind off 4 sts at beg of next 2 rows.

NEXT ROW: k2, k2tog, knit to last 4 sts, k2tog tbl, k2.

Working all dec as set, dec 1 st at each end of every alt row 3 times (54 [59, 64, 69] sts). Cont straight until armholes measure 6½ (7, 7½, 8)" (17 [18, 19, 20]cm) ending with a WS row.

SHOULDER AND NECK SHAPING

Bind off 6 (6, 7, 7) sts at beg of next 2 rows.

NEXT ROW: Bind off 6 (6, 6, 7) sts. Work until there are 5 (6, 6, 6) sts on right hand needle. Turn, then bind off rem sts.

Place center 20 (23, 26, 29) sts on a holder. Rejoin yarn and work to end.

NEXT ROW: Bind off 6 (6, 6, 7) sts.

Bind off rem sts.

FRONT

Work front same as back until armholes measure 5 (5½, 6, 6½)" (13 [14, 15, 17]cm), ending with a WS row.

NECK AND SHOULDER SHAPING

k22 (23, 24, 25) sts, turn. Place rem sts on a holder. Dec 1 st at neck edge of next and every foll alt row 4 times (17 [18, 19, 20] sts). Work 2 rows in stockinette. Bind off 6 (6, 7, 7) sts at armhole edge once, then bind off 6 (6, 6, 7) sts at armhole edge once. Bind off rem sts.

SLEEVES

With size US 7 (4.5mm) needles and CC, CO 36 (36, 40, 40) sts. Work in stockinette for 4 rows, then work in k2, p2 rib for 8 (8, 10, 10) rows.

Change to MC and size US 9 (5.5mm) needles. Working in stockinette, inc 1 st at each end of next and every foll sixth (5th, 5th, 5th) row 10 (12, 12, 14) times (58 [62, 66, 70] sts). Cont straight until sleeve measures 12 (13½, 15, 16)" (31 [33, 38, 41]cm) from cast-on edge, ending with a WS row.

Bind off 4 sts at beg of next 2 rows (52 [62, 66, 72] sts). Dec as follows, k2, k2tog, k to last 4 sts, k2tog tbl, k2, at each end of next and every foll alt row 5 (5, 6, 6) times, then every row 14 (16, 16, 18) times 12 [18, 20, 22] sts). Bind off rem sts.

TIP

When knitting with variegated yarn, alternate between two skeins to prevent the colors from pooling.

SHAPE SLEEVE CAPS

Bind off 4 sts at beg of next 2 rows.

NEXT ROW: k2, k2tog, knit to last 4 sts, k2tog tbl, k2.

Working all dec as set, dec 1 st each end of every foll alt row 5 times.

NEXT ROW: p2, p2tog tbl, purl to last 4 sts, p2tog, p2.

NEXT ROW: k2, k2tog, knit to last 4 sts, k2tog tbl, k2.

Working all dec as set, dec 1 st each end of every foll row 12 times (10 [14, 18, 22] sts). Bind off all sts.

FINISHING

Sew shoulder seams.

COLLAR

With RS facing, using 16" (41cm) size US 7 (4.5mm) circular needle and CC, k20 (23, 26, 29) sts from stitch holder at back of neck, pick up and knit 4 sts up left back neck, 13 (14, 13, 14) sts down left front neck, k10 (13, 16, 19) sts from stitch holder at front, pick up and k13 (14, 13, 14) sts up right front neck, and 4 sts down right back neck (64 [72, 76, 84] sts). Work 3 rnds in k2, p2 rib. Knit 2 rows. Bind off loosely.

Sew side and sleeve seams.

With size H crochet hook, work 1 rnd of slip stitch around bottom hem, then 1 round of single crochet. Weave in all ends.

measurements

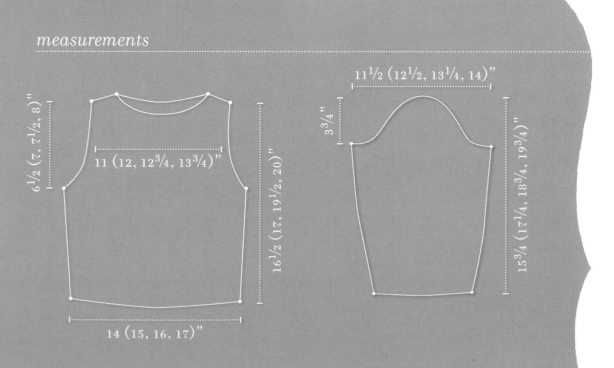

$6^{1}/_{2}$ (7, $7^{1}/_{2}$, 8)"

11 (12, $12^{3}/_{4}$, $13^{3}/_{4}$)"

$16^{1}/_{2}$ (17, $19^{1}/_{2}$, 20)"

14 (15, 16, 17)"

$11^{1}/_{2}$ ($12^{1}/_{2}$, $13^{1}/_{4}$, 14)"

$3^{3}/_{4}$"

$15^{3}/_{4}$ ($17^{1}/_{4}$, $18^{3}/_{4}$, $19^{3}/_{4}$)"

helpful INFORMATION

KNITTING ABBREVIATIONS

alt	ALTERNATE
beg	BEGINNING
bo	BIND OFF
cc	CONTRAST COLOR
cn	CABLE NEEDLE
co	CAST ON
dec	DECREASE
dpn(s)	DOUBLE POINTED NEEDLE(S)
foll	FOLLOWING
inc	INCREASE
k	KNIT
k2tog	KNIT 2 TOGETHER
k2tog tbl	KNIT 2 TOGETHER THROUGH BACK LOOP
m1	MAKE ONE INCREASE
mc	MAIN COLOR
p	PURL
p2tog	PURL 2 TOGETHER
p2tog tbl	PURL 2 TOGETHER THROUGH BACK LOOP
pm	PLACE MARKER
psso	PASS SLIPPED STITCH OVER
rem	REMAINING
rs	RIGHT SIDE
rep	REPEAT
sl	SLIP
ssk	SLIP, SLIP, KNIT
st(s)	STITCH(ES)
ws	WRONG SIDE
yo	YARN OVER

KNITTING NEEDLE CONVERSIONS

diameter (mm)	US size	suggested yarn weight
2	0	LACE WEIGHT
2.25	1	LACE AND FINGERING WEIGHT
2.75	2	LACE AND FINGERING WEIGHT
3.25	3	FINGERING AND SPORT WEIGHT
3.5	4	FINGERING AND SPORT WEIGHT
3.75	5	DK AND SPORT WEIGHT
4	6	DK, SPORT AND ARAN/WORSTED WEIGHT
4.5	7	ARAN/WORSTED WEIGHT
5	8	ARAN/WORSTED AND HEAVY WORSTED WEIGHT
5.5	9	ARAN/WORSTED, HEAVY WORSTED AND CHUNKY/BULKY
6	10	CHUNKY/BULKY
6.5	10½	CHUNKY/BULKY AND SUPER BULKY
8	11	CHUNKY/BULKY AND SUPER BULKY
9	13	SUPER BULKY
10	15	SUPER BULKY
12.75	17	SUPER BULKY
15	19	SUPER BULKY
	36	SUPER BULKY

SUBSTITUTING YARNS

At the time of publication, all of the yarns used in this book were still being produced. However, a yarn company may decide to discontinue a particular yarn or color with little or no notice.

When it comes to substituting yarns, gauge is everything. Check the label to make sure that the horizontal gauge (number of stitches per inch) is the same as the required gauge in the pattern that you are working with. To determine yardage, do a web search on the yarn listed in the pattern. Multiply yardage by the number of skeins to determine exactly how much yarn you will need to complete your project. It is best to purchase all of the yarn at once, as it may be difficult to match your dye lot at a later date. Because every knitter knits in a different way it is always necessary to knit a swatch to determine that you are getting the proper gauge, thus ensuring that the final measurements of your project will be as specified.

GLOSSARY
knitting and crochet terms and techniques

CABLES

Although cables may seem difficult, they're really quite simple. To create a cable, slip (sl) the number of stitches indicated in the pattern onto a cable needle (cn) and hold the cable needle at the front or back of the work, as directed. Simply ignore the cable needle and knit the number of stitches indicated in the pattern from the left-hand needle. Rejoin the stitches on the cable needle to the main stitches by knitting them off of the cable needle. Holding the cable needle to the front or back of your work determines the way the cable twists.

CABLE NEEDLE (CN)

A cable needle is a small hook- or U-shaped needle that is pointed on either end. Select a cable needle that is close to the diameter of the needles you use for the project.

CASTING ON (CO)

Casting on is the term for creating the number of stitches needed for the first row of any project. There are several methods for casting on—for the projects in this book, you may use the method you're most comfortable with.

CASTING ON WITH DOUBLE-POINTED NEEDLES

If one of your double-pointed needles can accommodate the full number of stitches, cast all of the stitches onto one needle. If your needles are shorter, you may opt to cast all of the stitches onto one longer straight needle. Once all of the stitches have been cast on, divide them evenly between four of the dpn. To divide the stitches, hold the needle with the cast-on stitches in your left hand, as if to knit. Using a dpn, insert the tip of the needle into the first stitch as if to purl. Slip the stitch to the right-hand needle. Continue to slip stitches as if to purl until the stitches are divided evenly over four needles. The remaining dpn is for knitting.

CROCHET STITCHES

Some projects in this book use a small crocheted border as a finishing technique. You don't need to know much about crochet, just knowing these basic stitches will do.

SLIP STITCH CROCHET

On right side of fabric, with edge facing away from you, insert hook into top edge of stitch, wrap yarn over hook and pull through fabric. * Insert hook into next stitch, wrap yarn over hook, pull through the fabric and through the loop on hook. Rep from * to create a border as desired.

SINGLE CROCHET

On right side of fabric, with edge facing away from you, insert hook into top edge of stitch, wrap yarn over hook and pull through fabric, wrap yarn over hook and pull through loop. * Insert hook into next stitch, wrap yarn over hook and pull through both loops on hook. Rep from * as desired.

DECREASES

There are many different ways to decrease the number of stitches on your needles. You can use a decrease method that doesn't show up in the finished knitted fabric, or you can make the decreases a part of the design by choosing a method that creates an obvious pattern in the knitted fabric.

KNIT TWO TOGETHER (K2TOG)

Knitting two stitches together as one (k2tog) is a simple way to decrease the number of stitches in a row. Simply slip your right-hand needle through the first two stitches on the left-hand needle from front to back, as for a regular knit stitch. Knit the two stitches as one, creating one less stitch.

PURL TWO TOGETHER (P2TOG)

Slip your right-hand needle through the first two stitches on the left-hand needle from back to front, as for a regular purl stitch. Purl the two stitches as one, creating one less stitch.

KNIT OR PURL TWO TOGETHER THROUGH BACK LOOP (K2TOG TBL OR P2TOG TBL)

Insert the right needle into the back loops of the first two stitches on the left-hand needle. Wrap the yarn and knit or purl as usual.

SLIP, SLIP, KNIT (SSK)

To create a left-slanting decrease, slip the first stitch as if to knit, slip the second stitch as if to knit, and then bring the right needle through both stitches from front to back and knit them together.

INCREASES

There are lots of different ways to increase the number of stitches in a given row. If the pattern simply says inc 1, you choose the method of increasing that works best for you.

KNIT ONE IN FRONT AND BACK (K1FB)

An easy way to increase is to knit one in the front and back of a stitch (k1fb). To make this type of increase, simply insert your right-hand needle into the next stitch on the left-hand needle and knit the stitch, keeping the stitch on the left-hand needle instead of sliding it off. Then bring your right hand needle around to the back, knit into the back loop of the same stitch, and slip both stitches off the needle.

MAKE ONE (M1)

With your right-hand needle, pick up the bar between two stitches from the back to front, and place it on the left-hand needle, then knit it through the back loop.

INTARSIA

At each color change, yarns must be wrapped around each other at the back of the work to prevent holes in the fabric. You may work with separate skeins, with yarn wound on bobbins, or with very long strands of yarn. Take time to untangle your strands every few rows.

MATTRESS STITCH

Unless otherwise indicated, mattress stitch is used for all seams in this book. Mattress stitch creates an invisible seam by replicating the stitches on either side of the seam using a darning needle and the same yarn used to create the knitted piece.

To create mattress stitch on stockinette pieces, work on the right side of the fabric, bringing the neede up between the two legs of a v stitch on one piece, down through the front of the fabric outside of the v stitch on the other piece of fabric, under both legs of the same stitch, up through the fabric on the other outside of that same stitch, then down through the right side of the first piece of fabric at the same point where you brought the needle up for the first part of the stitch. Repeat along the entire length of the seam. See a reference guide for working mattress stitch on garter stitch.

PICKING UP STITCHES

To pick up a stitch, insert the tip of one needle through the side of a stitch from front to back. Leaving about a 3"–4" (8cm–10cm) tail, wrap yarn around the needle as you would for a regular knit stitch. Bring the yarn through the stitch, creating a loop on your needle. This loop is the first picked-up stitch. Continue to pick up the number of stitches required, making sure to space them evenly.

PLACING A MARKER (PM)

Sometimes a pattern calls for you to place a marker (pm). Markers are generally small plastic rings that slide onto a needle and rest in between stitches, marking a certain spot. If you don't have markers on hand, cut small pieces of scrap yarn in a contrasting color. Tie the scrap yarn around the needle in the indicated spot in a loose knot. Move the marker from one needle to the other when you come to it. Continue as usual.

PLACING STITCHES ON A HOLDER

Most sweater patterns require that you place some of the front and back neck stitches onto a holder as you bind off the shoulder stitches. You may buy a stitch holder and slide the stitches onto it, or just use a piece of scrap yarn in a contrasting color. The stitches will be picked back up at the end to make a neckband.

STITCHES

EYELETS

Eyelets are small, decorative holes in knitted fabric. Create them with regular yarn overs. Remember to make an equal number of decreases on the following row so the knitted fabric doesn't grow exponentially.

GARTER RIDGE

Garter stitch is created by knitting every row. However, if you'd like to add just a bit of texture to punctuate a smoother stitch like stockinette with garter stitch, make sure to knit two rows to create a garter ridge.

GLOSSARY

continued

RIBBING

To create ribbing, simply alternate between knitting and purling. You can create a one-by-one rib, a two-by-two rib, a one-by-three rib...etc.! Ribbing is often used for sweater waistbands, cuffs and neckbands, and also for hat brims.

SEED STITCH

Seed stitch is a simple stitch that creates an interesting texture. Seed stitch is worked by knitting all purl stitches and purling all knit stitches. Here's how it works:

FOR AN ODD NUMBER OF STITCHES

ROW 1: * k1, p1; rep from * until last st, k1.

Rep Row 1.

FOR AN EVEN NUMBER OF STITCHES

ROW 1: * k1, p1*, rep from * until end of row.

ROW 2: * p1, k1; rep from * until end of row.

REP ROWS 1 and 2.

STOCKINETTE STITCH

To create stockinette stitch, knit on the right side and purl on the wrong side. If you're knitting in the round, knitting every row produces effortless stockinette with no purling.

YARN OVER (YO)

A yarn over is as easy as it sounds. When you come to a yarn over in the pattern, simply wrap the working yarn around the right-hand needle and continue knitting as usual. On the following row, you will knit or purl the wrapped yarn, creating an extra stitch and also an attractive eyelet hole in the knitted fabric. Because a yarn over creates a new stitch, a row with yarn overs is often combined with decreases.

WORKING IN THE ROUND

Before you begin, make sure that your circular needles are a bit shorter than the diameter of your project. Simply cast on the requisite number of stitches just as you would on straight needles. Also make sure the stitches are not twisted. Hold the needle with the tail dangling from it in your left hand. Push the stitches to the end of the needle. Hold the needle with the working yarn in your right hand, pushing the first stitches to the end of that needle. Insert the tip of the right needle into the first stitch on the left needle from front to back. Wrap the working yarn around the right needle and knit your first stitch. Voilá, you're connected! After that, knit every row to produce stockinette stitch.

resource
GUIDE

ARTYARNS
39 Westmoreland Ave.
White Plains, NY
phone: 914.428.0333
www.artyarns.com

**ARAUCANIA, DEBBIE BLISS,
NORO & PATAGONIA YARNS**
Distributed by Knitting
Fever International
PO Box 336
315 Bayview Ave.
Amityville, NY 11701
phone: 516.546.3600
www.knittingfever.com

**LANAKNITS HEMP
FOR KNITTING**
Ste. 3B, 320 Vernon St.
Nelson BC V1L 4E4
phone: 888.301.0011
www.hempforknitting.com

LION BRAND YARN CO
www.lionbrand.com

LORNA'S LACES YARNS
4229 N. Honore St.
Chicago, IL 60613
www.lornaslaces.net

PEACE FLEECE
475 Porterfield Rd.
Porter, Maine 04068
phone: 800.482.2841
www.peacefleece.com

ROWAN YARNS
Westminster Fibers, Inc.
4 Townsend West, Unit 8
Nashua, NH 03063
phone: 800.445.9276

**SOUTH WEST TRADING
COMPANY**
918 S. Park Ln., Ste. 102
Tempe, AZ 85281
phone: 480.894.1818

FILATURA DI CROSA
Distributed by Tahki Stacy
Charles, Inc.
70-30 80th St. Building 36
Ridgewood, NY 11385
www.tahkistacycharles.com

knitting
INSPIRATIONS

If you like to knit, it's very likely you enjoy poring over pattern books and magazines, and you may even have discovered the pleasures of the knitting blog. Below are a few of the places I regularly go for knitting inspiration.

MAGAZINES

In the last few years there has been an upsurge in the publication of knitting magazines. If you do a little sleuthing on the Web or a little browsing in your favorite local bookstore, you'll find a wide selection of knitting publications. There's something for every kind of knitting taste and skill level. Here are a few of my favorite knitting mags.

Rowan Magazine

Long an industry standard, Rowan is equally well known for its luxurious yarns and high-fashion knitting patterns. Because of the length of time involved in putting together a knitting publication, it is almost impossible to keep designs current with what is on the runways. Rowan comes closer than most knitting magazines, giving us some of the hottest designs around.

Vintage *Vogue Knitting Magazines* from the 1950s–1960s

What can you say? *Vogue* is always en vogue. Their vintage patterns are painstaking and exquisite (imagine knitting a two piece boucle suit on size 2 needles). Check eBay for vintage editions from the 1940s through the 1960s.

Italian Vogue

For years, *Italian Vogue* has been the ne plus ultra of *Vogue Magazines*. Its cutting-edge fashion and photography sets it miles apart from its competitors. If you want to know what's white hot in fashion, this is where you'll find it!

i-D

This super cool, London-based magazine always has its finger on the pulse of what's new and interesting in art, film, fashion and music worldwide.

KNITTING BOOKS

Knitting books are growing ever more beautiful, entertaining and functional. Every knitter should have a well-rounded selection of books, from the purely inspirational to the practical reference book. Here are a few of the books on my shelves that get repeated thumbing through.

Vogue Knitting: The Ultimate Knitting Book

This reference book is a must-have for every knitter, new and old. From basic beginner's techniques to invaluable information on finishing techniques and advanced knitting skills like colorwork, this book has everything any knitter could need, including in-depth information on correcting your knitting snafus.

Stitch 'N Bitch
BY DEBBIE STOLLER

This fun-to-read book has an extensive how-to knitting guide that even the totally new knitter will find easy to follow. It features hip designs by knitters-turned-designers who are tuned in to what people really want to knit.

The Knitter's Book of Finishing Techniques
BY NANCIE M. WISEMAN

Finishing can make or break a completed project. This excellent reference book provides photos and detailed instructions for a wide variety of finishing techniques.

BLOGS

Watch out, blogs can be dangerously addictive. There's an ever-growing online community of knitters, and they always want to share what's on their needles and what's going on in their lives. Blogs are a great place to get inspiration, patterns and often a few laughs. Here are some of my favorites to visit.

Art for Housewives
WWW.HOUSEWIFE.SPLINDER.COM/

Artist Cynthia Korzekwa devotes this website to her massive compilation of links to outsider art, recycled craft and domestic arts. If you want to learn how people are reusing, recycling and reinventing, this is the place to go!

Purl Jam

PURLJAM.TYPEPAD.COM

Tracy Stewart, more commonly know to the knitting universe as Rock Chick, is the sassy voice behind this clever knitting blog. Her amusing posts run the gamut from discussing finished and unfinished knitting projects to chronicling her virgin adventure with cleaning raw fleece. Her blog also contains links to some of the coolest knitting on the web.

Strikker

OBSESSIVEKNITTING.BLOGSPOT.COM

It's true. The woman who runs this blog knits obsessively. Go to her blog if you want to a) be inspired or b) be depressed by your own complete lack of productivity.

Mason Dixon Knitting

WWW.MASONDIXONKNITTING.COM

Kay Gardiner and Ann Shayne post back and forth to each other on their blog, bringing warmth and good knitting to the online (and offline) knitting community. They have recently published a knitting book of their own, *Mason-Dixon Knitting*.

Pinku

PINKUROCKS.TYPEPAD.COM/PINKU

Katherine Mok is an Australian knitter living in Tokyo, Japan. As the founder of the Tokyo SnB, she provides an insider's view into the vibrant Tokyo knitting scene. Her blog also features great pictures and stories from her travel adventures.

Knit and Tonic

KNITANDTONIC.TYPEPAD.COM/KNITANDTONIC/

Wendy Bernard of southern California learned to knit when she was eight, but didn't pick up needles again until she was pregnant with her daughter four years ago. Her witty posts and cool projects have won her a devoted following of readers who tune in daily to catch up on her knitting adventures.

Bound by My Hook and Needles Too

WWW.BOUNDBYMYHOOK.BLOGSPOT.COM/

Erica B, a stay-at-home mom from Birmingham, Alabama, is quite the prolific knitter and crocheter. Whether creating her own designs or modifying existing patterns, she whips up more amazingly beautiful projects in a month than I could even dream of. Does this woman ever sleep?

The Sartorialist

WWW.THESARTORIALIST.BLOGSPOT.COM

The mysterious man behind The Sartorialist stops stylish New Yorkers on the street and asks if he can photograph them. The result: Daily photos of some of the most creative and innovative dressers in the world.

WEB SITES

There are all sorts of knit-centric Web sites out there now, as well as tons of non-knitting sites from which to draw great inspiration. Here are a few I visit often.

Camilla Engman

WWW.CAMILLAENGMAN.COM

Camilla Engman is a Swedish artist and crocheter whose whimsical work always makes me look for a way to introduce a bit more humor into my designs. Her highly sought after crocheted characters are an absolute delight!

The Quilts of Gee's Bend

WWW.QUILTSOFGEESBEND.COM/QUILTS/

The astounding work of the Gee's Bend Quilters is the foundation for my design and color aesthetic. Their handiwork, as well as their personal stories, come together to create a rich tapestry of inspiration. Seeing the beauty they produce using limited materials is sure to serve as motivation to create something from even the smallest stash!

Whip Up

WWW.WHIPUP.NET

Whip Up is a collective of artists and crafters from around the world who post daily on everything craft. From knitting to sewing to ceramics, they have all the bases covered when it comes to info, techniques, and who's who in the world of handmade art and crafts.

INDEX

check out these other fabulous
KNITTING AND CROCHET TITLES FROM F+W PUBLICATIONS, INC.

DomiKNITrix
BY JENNIFER STAFFORD

Once you know the joys of disciplined knitting, you'll never look back. Let experienced knitter Jennifer Stafford help you whip your stitches into shape. This book features a no-nonsense, comprehensive guide to essential knitting operations and finishing techniques. In the second half of the book, you'll put your knitting know-how to the test with patterns for over 20 handknit projects to wear and gift, including a halter "bra-let," a contoured zipper vest, a Jughead hat, icon sweaters and even a knitted mohawk. Plus much, much more.

ISBN-13: 978-1-58180-853-7
ISBN-10: 1-58180-853-4
FLEXIBIND CASE, 240 PAGES, Z0171

Crochet Squared
BY MARSHA A. POLK

If you can crochet a simple scarf, you can make any of the stylish and sophisticated body wraps and accessories featured in *Crochet Squared*. Each of the over 20 projects in the book is based on a simple square or rectangle shape, allowing even beginning crocheters to make gorgeous works of art. *Crochet Squared* takes crochet out of the time warp and brings it into the new millennium. Marsha Polk's striking use of color and novelty yarns makes these for stunning and sophisticated projects. You'll also find a practical guide to basic crochet techniques.

ISBN-13: 978-1-58180-833-9
ISBN-10: 1-58180-833-X
PAPERBACK, 128 PAGES, 33507

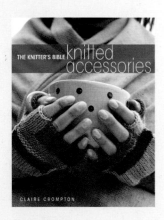

Knitter's Bible: Knitted Accessories
BY CLAIRE CROMPTON

This collection of over 30 stylish knitted accessories for every season is sure to please knitters of all skill levels. Projects range from simple scarves and mittens to eye-catching hats and ponchos. With easy-to-follow techniques, detailed photography and plenty of variations, this guide is a must-have for knitters who want to create their own accessories or give a personalized gift.

ISBN-13: 978-0-7153-2327-4
ISBN-10: 0-7153-2327-X
PAPERBACK, 128 PAGES, Z0465

Not Tonight Darling, I'm Knitting
BY BETSY HOSEGOOD

Knitting is more than just a simple craft, it's a great way to be social. This glamorous and gifty book appeals to knitters everywhere to pick up their needles and join the fun. Inside, you'll find real-life knitting stories, tips and advice for shopping for the perfect yarn, a fresh look at the history of knitting and knitting fashion, knitting testimonies from celebrities, and more. This book is a must-have for anyone who loves to knit.

ISBN-13: 978-0-7153-2407-3
ISBN-10: 0-7153-2407-1
HARDBACK, 128 PAGES, 41900

These books and other fine F+W Publications, Inc. titles are available at your local craft retailer, bookstore or from online suppliers.